Understanding Special
Educational Needs

'Michael Farrell has produced a book which should be essential reading for all newly qualified teachers or those currently in initial teacher education. He provides a clear pathway through the many legislative demands upon teachers and supports this with well articulated examples of how good practice can influence standards and achievements.'

Professor Richard Rose, University College, Northampton

Teachers need to be fully equipped to respond to diversity in today's classrooms now more than ever before. The *Professional Standards for Qualified Teacher Status* and *Induction Standards* are now the driving force behind initial teacher education, and students will need to demonstrate their competence against these, and in particular, their understanding of Special Educational Needs in today's inclusive classrooms.

Each chapter of this indispensable text explores an important topic within SEN and directly relates it to the competencies, making it an essential course companion. Chapters cover essential topics relating to the *Special Educational Needs Code of Practice*, school policy, literacy and numeracy, ICT, emotional and behavioural difficulties and working with parents.

Detailed referencing will lead students to pursue more detailed individual texts which address many of the issues in greater depth. This is an ideal, highly accessible text for student and newly qualified teachers who need a reliable introduction to today's vital issues within Special Educational Needs.

Michael Farrell is a special education consultant working with LEAs, universities, schools and others. He has previously written *Key Issues for Primary Schools* and *Key Issues for Secondary Schools* both published by RoutledgeFalmer.

Understanding Special Educational Needs

A guide for student teachers

P 1B
P 25

Michael Farrell

RoutledgeFalmer
Taylor & Francis Group

LONDON AND NEW YORK

First published 2003
by RoutledgeFalmer
11 New Fetter Lane, London EC4P 4EE

Simultaneously published in the USA and Canada
by RoutledgeFalmer
29 West 35th Street, New York, NY 10001

RoutledgeFalmer is an imprint of the Taylor & Francis Group

© 2003 Michael Farrell

Typeset in Times and Gill by BC Typesetting, Bristol
Printed and bound in Great Britain by
TJ International Ltd, Padstow, Cornwall

British Library Cataloguing in Publication Data
A catalogue record for this book is available from the British Library

Library of Congress Cataloging in Publication Data
A catalog record for this book is on request

ISBN 0–415–30822–4 (hbk)
ISBN 0–415–30823–2 (pbk)

To my dear friend Peter Crisell
With warm affection

Contents

Foreword   ix
Acknowledgements   xi
List of abbreviations   xiii

Introduction   1

1 Defining and distinguishing special educational
  needs   10

2 Inclusion   24

3 The *Special Educational Needs Code of Practice*   36

4 Equal opportunities and local SEN policy   47

5 Raising educational achievement and the use of
  Individual Education Plans   57

6 Literacy and numeracy   67

7 Information and communications technology   78

8 Resources   89

9 Emotional, behavioural and social difficulties   98

10 Developing one's teaching 109

11 Assessment, recording and reporting 121

12 Partners and participants 130

Appendix 1: Useful addresses 143
Appendix 2: Internet addresses 145
Glossary 147
Bibliography 149
Author index 157
Subject index 158

Foreword

A great deal has been written in the past ten years or so about the organisation and management of inclusive approaches in education for children experiencing learning difficulties and disabilities (collectively referred to here as 'special educational needs – SEN'). A great deal of this work has been undertaken with a focus upon strategic direction at a national level, government policy and its ongoing impact on whole schools. Much of the statutory guidance being issued in England, for instance, retains a focus on the bureaucracy of inclusion, and offers a somewhat managerialist approach which seems to deny the crucial role of the teacher as the real facilitator of the process. It therefore seems vital that a return is made to a focus on the work that teachers actually 'do' in classrooms. This is the heartbeat of the movement towards inclusive education for SEN.

Emphasising a teacher's role at the core of SEN and inclusion brings with it many benefits, both intrinsic and pragmatic. The classroom practitioner who has reflected upon their own 'personal theory' regarding inclusion will be in a better position to contribute to wider developments in the whole school and to influence those colleagues who may be 'inclusion-resistant'. One of the most effective ways of doing this is by becoming a 'model' of good practice. Moreover, teachers who ask tough questions about their own pedagogy become far more resilient supporters of inclusive approaches, in that this kind of interrogation enables important parallels to be drawn between 'good' and 'inclusive' teaching. Finally, an emphasis on the individual ensures that the primacy of the social relationships between teacher and child is maintained.

Any positioning of the classroom teacher at the heart of developing good inclusive practice for SEN has to come with a major conditional clause. A positive and enabling framework has to be secured in initial teacher training (ITT) so that, on completion of any course leading to qualified teacher status, a new entrant to the profession will have had opportunities to establish an initial repertoire of skills and knowledge about SEN. Such opportunities would also include the process of developing an understanding of what 'inclusion' actually means in practical terms. Both issues remain contentious, in that even in 2003 many teachers complain that coverage of SEN in their training has been marginal, a situation which has been noted by many commentators (Garner, 2000; 2001; Robertson, 2000; Rose, 2002).

The importance of Michael Farrell's book within the context I have described should be clear. He has provided a comprehensive map of the key issues to be encountered by new teachers. At one level, as a teacher trainer, I regard this as an essential survival resource for that potentially stressful (though exhilarating) period of initial training and a subsequent first appointment. The reader will find within these pages a 'kit-bag' of SEN and inclusion-related materials, which has been carefully assembled to lend coherence and order to a bewildering array of professional requirements. Moreover, his account will find a secure place in the personal libraries of training providers.

Second, the contents of this book form a suitable baseline from which students and new teachers can begin the process of developing a personal 'position' in respect of SEN and inclusion. Critical reflection – asking the difficult questions of ourselves in the interrogation of our practice – lies at the very core of the development of effective teaching, and it is essential to meeting the longer-term educational needs of children experiencing SEN. Michael Farrell's work here provides abundant opportunities for students and tutors alike to engage in this process.

All students and new teachers also need to be supported in the development of personal, 'living theories' about SEN and inclusion. This will, in part, be based upon knowledge of policies and a set of core skills and teaching approaches. But a further, significant contribution is likely to be made by the individual personality, outlook and humanitarian stance of the teacher him or herself. This book strikes a healthy balance between these pivotal matters. The beneficiaries of such a considered approach are likely to be all children in truly inclusive classroom settings.

Professor Philip Garner, *Nottingham Trent University*

Acknowledgements

I am most grateful to Ms Kate Coveney, newly qualified teacher and to Gail Treml of the Special Educational Needs Division, Department for Education and Skills, for reading the manuscript and making helpful suggestions. The staff of Routledge Falmer were exemplary in their support and I am particularly grateful to Alison Foyle and Jude Exley.

The inclusion of an address anywhere in the book does not indicate that members of that organisation agree with or endorse mention of their organisation. The address is a source of further information and does not necessarily indicate that any documents listed in references or further reading can be obtained from the address.

Where references are given to a publication prepared by an organisation, the name of the organisation as it was at the time of the publication is given. For example, the present Department for Education and Skills has had several previous titles so a publication made when the Department was, say, the Department of Education is cited with that earlier Department name.

The views expressed in *Understanding Special Educational Needs* are personal. Any shortcomings of the book are, of course, entirely my own.

Abbreviations

ADHD	attention deficit hyperactivity disorder
ASD	autistic spectrum disorder
BDA	British Dyslexia Association
BECTA	British Educational Communications and Technology Agency
BILD	British Institute of Learning Difficulties
BSP	behaviour support plan
CATs	cognitive ability tests
CCP	Child Care Plan
COP	Code of Practice
CSIE	Centre for Studies in Inclusive Education
DfES	Department for Education and Skills
EAL	English as an additional language
EBSD	emotional, behavioural and social difficulties
EP	educational psychologist
EPS	educational psychology service
EWO	educational welfare officer
EWS	Education Welfare Service
HI	hearing impairment
ICT	information and communications technology
IEP	Individual Education Plan
INSET	in-service education and training
IPSEA	Independent Panel for Special Educational Advice
ITT	initial teacher training
LEA	local education authority
LSA	learning support assistant
MLD	moderate learning difficulties
NASEN	National Association for Special Educational Needs
NC	National Curriculum

NQT	newly qualified teacher
PD	physical disability
PMLD	profound and multiple learning difficulties
PPO	Parent Partnership Officer
PRU	Pupil Referral Unit
PSHE	personal, social and health education
PSP	Pastoral Support Programme
QCA	Qualifications and Curriculum Authority
QTS	qualified teacher status
SALT	speech and language therapist
SEN	special educational needs
SENCO	Special Educational Needs Co-ordinator
SENDA	Special Educational Needs and Disability Act 2001
SENDIST	Special Educational Needs and Disability Tribunal
SLD	severe learning difficulties
SNO	special needs officer
SpLD	specific learning difficulties
STP	short-term plans
TA	teaching assistant
TTA	Teacher Training Agency
VI	visual impairment

Introduction

If the succinct advice on making an effective speech, 'Stand up, put up, shut up' is true, then the present chapter is equivalent to standing up. I will try to explain the rationale of the book; say who are the intended readers and introduce the *Professional Standards for Qualified Teacher Status* and the *Induction Standards*. The chapter will briefly consider how the standards approach may be used to allow flexibility and innovation in training.

The rationale of the book

This book indicates how aspects of government-supported standards for teacher training and induction might be understood as they relate to special educational needs (SEN). It concentrates on the two major publications concerning SEN:

1 *Professional Standards for Qualified Teacher Status* (Teacher Training Agency, 2002a);
2 the *Induction Standards for Newly Qualified Teachers* (Teacher Training Agency, 2002b).

Hereafter, these two documents will be referred to respectively as the *QTS Standards* and the *Induction Standards*.

The *QTS Standards* set out the values, knowledge and understanding and teaching that must be demonstrated for a trainee teacher to be awarded qualified teacher status (QTS). The *Induction Standards* lay down similar requirements that must be met if a newly qualified teacher (NQT) is to successfully participate in and complete the induction process.

While these requirements are central, it is sometimes necessary to go beyond them as they are, after all, the minimum expected for qualified teacher status and successful NQT induction.

Intended readership

I hope this book will be helpful to the following readers:

- students undergoing initial teacher training (ITT) and those who work with them;
- NQTs and those working with them;
- all teachers wishing to review some of the key issues relating to SEN;
- overseas students and practitioners wishing to gain an overview of some key issues in SEN in England;
- head teachers (as a reference book).

The text applies in particular to maintained primary and secondary schools in England whether they are community, aided or foundation and to non-maintained special schools. It should also be of interest to staff in independent schools.

A continuum of professional development

The *QTS Standards* (Teacher Training Agency, 2002a, p. 2) may be seen as relating to a continuum of professional development comprising:

- initial teacher training;
- the induction period;
- professional development and performance management.

ITT is the foundation for subsequent professional and career development. The induction period involves the NQT building on strengths identified in initial training and working on areas identified (by him or herself and those working with him or her) as priorities for future professional development. Continuing professional development and performance management build on the foundations laid by initial teacher training and NQT induction.

The Professional Standards for Qualified Teacher Status

The 'Professional Standards for Qualified Teacher Status' are included in a document which also specifies the Requirements for initial teacher training providers. The document *Qualifying to Teach: Professional Standards for Qualified Teacher Status* and *Requirements for Initial Teacher Training* (Teacher Training Agency, 2002a) therefore sets out:

- the Secretary of State's standards which must be met by trainee teachers before they can be awarded QTS (the QTS Standards);
- the requirements for training providers and those who make recommendations for the award of QTS (the Requirements).

One cannot pick and choose from the QTS Standards for it is made clear that only the trainee teacher who has met all of the QTS Standards will be awarded QTS. The document is to be used to establish a common framework of expectations and is intended to promote high professional standards for all those in teaching.

ITT is not seen as an end in itself but as the beginning of the process of professional development. The QTS Standards and Requirements should ensure that teachers have the necessary subject knowledge and teaching expertise and that they are well prepared for the wider professional demands of being a teacher. The QTS Standards should also, in the words of the then Secretary of State and the Chief Executive of the Teacher Training Agency, 'ensure that training tackles issues such as behaviour management and social inclusion well' (Teacher Training Agency, 2002a, p. 1). It is recognised that teachers have an influence through the following:

- the curriculum taught;
- their own behaviour, attitudes and values;
- their relationships with pupils;
- their interest in pupils.

(Ibid., p. 2)

Teaching requires 'care, mutual respect and well placed optimism' (ibid., p. 2). It also requires:

- knowledge and practical skills;
- the ability to make informed judgements;
- the ability to balance various elements (pressures and challenge, practice and creativity, interest and effort);
- an understanding of how children learn and develop;
- recognition of the contribution of others to children's learning in school and at home and in the local community.

(Ibid., p. 2)

The QTS Standards are 'outcome statements' representing expectations and setting out the minimum legal requirement (ibid., p. 3). They lay down what, in order to be awarded QTS, a trainee must know, understand, and be able to do. They are organised in three inter-related sections describing the criteria for the awards:

- professional values and practice;
- knowledge and understanding;
- teaching.

Under 'professional values and practice' are outlined the 'attitudes and commitment' expected of anyone qualifying as a teacher (these are derived from the professional code of the General Teaching Council for England).

In the section on 'knowledge and understanding' the requirements are that these teachers have a clear understanding of how all pupils should progress and what teachers should expect pupils to achieve.

Regarding 'teaching', the QTS Standards concern the following skills:

- planning;
- monitoring and assessment;
- teaching;
- class management.

Given that the QTS Standards represent a minimum legal requirement, ITT providers may offer additional training to develop the trainee teacher's knowledge and skills. In training for the primary phase, trainers may choose to provide additional training by, for example, offering training in a specialist area of study such as the teaching of pupils with SEN (Ibid., p. 3).

The *Handbook of Guidance on QTS Standards and ITT Requirements* helps explain the Standards and Requirements (Teacher Training Agency, 2002c). It comprises two sections. The first gives guidance on the Standards for the award of QTS, while the second covers the Requirements for initial teacher training. This book takes account of the *Handbook* guidance.

The relationship between the QTS Standards and the Induction Standards

A guidance document, *The Induction Period for Newly Qualified Teachers* (Department for Education and Skills, 2002) includes in an appendix an earlier version of the Induction Standards. The document describes the arrangements for every NQT to complete a period of induction should they wish to work in a maintained school or in a non-maintained special school in England. It gives indications of how the head teacher and other school staff should support, monitor and assess NQTs during their first year of teaching and covers appeal arrangements should the teacher fail the final assessment.

The Induction Standards have subsequently been developed from the version that originally appeared in the above guidance document. Pending any amendments following consultation, the new Induction Standards (Teacher Training Agency, 2002b) will apply to teachers starting NQT induction from September 2003. In the present book, I use these new Standards. The Induction Standards require that the NQT has done the following:

- continued to meet the QTS Standards consistently in teaching at the school;
- met all the Induction Standards.

The Induction Standards build on particular aspects of the QTS Standards. They do this by requiring NQTs to work independently in areas where, during initial training, it was assumed they would have the support of an experienced teacher; and by focusing on aspects of professional practice which can be better developed during employment as a qualified teacher, and over a longer period of teaching than is normally available during initial training.

Below, the *Induction Standards* are set out in full except for a reference to the national numeracy test. It will be noticed that in subsequent chapters, the *QTS Standards* and the related *Handbook* are quoted at the beginning of each chapter while the *Induction Standards* are only occasionally quoted. This is because the *Induction Standards* include that the *QTS Standards* continue to be met so it is important for NQTs to continue to refer to the *QTS Standards*. Also, the *NQT Standards* are much shorter and can be referred to below as the reader requires.

The Induction Standards

To meet the Induction Standards, NQTs should, by the end of the induction period, demonstrate all of the following.

Professional Values and Practice

They continue to meet the requirements of the Professional Values and Practice section of the Standards for the Award of QTS, and build on these by taking an increasingly independent and proactive role in improving their own practice and improving practice across the school. Specifically, they:

(a)   actively contribute to and share responsibly in the corporate life of the school in which they are employed;

(b)   seek and use opportunities to improve their own teaching, setting objectives for improvement, planning and taking action to meet these, and reviewing their progress against them;

(c)   are able to contribute to the development of other adults in the school;

(d)   contribute to the sharing of effective practice in the school;

(e)   use ICT effectively to support their wider professional role.

Knowledge and Understanding

They continue to meet the requirements of the Knowledge and Understanding section of the Standards for the Award of QTS, and build on these by:

(f) identifying areas in which they need to add to and develop their subject and professional knowledge and understanding in order to teach more effectively in their current post, and taking steps to address these needs.

Teaching

They continue to meet the requirements of the Teaching section of the Standards for the Award of QTS, and build on these by demonstrating increasing responsibility and independence in their teaching and when working with other adults, including parents. Specifically, they:

Planning, Expectations and Targets

(g) plan effectively, where applicable, to meet the needs of pupils with Special Educational Needs, with or without statements, and in consultation with the SENCO contribute to the preparation, implementation, monitoring and review of Individual Education Plans or the equivalent;

Monitoring and Assessment

(h) take responsibility for identifying appropriate monitoring and assessment strategies to evaluate pupils' progress and use this information, along with other performance data, to improve their own planning and teaching and raise the achievement of boys and girls from all ethnic groups;

(i) assess pupils' progress accurately and independently using, as relevant, the Early Learning Goals, National Curriculum level descriptions, criteria from national qualifications, the requirements of Awarding Bodies, National Curriculum and Foundation Stage assessment frameworks or objectives from the national strategies;

(j) liaise effectively with parents or carers on pupils' progress and achievements;

Teaching and Class Management

(k) independently differentiate their teaching to meet the needs of pupils, including, where appropriate:

- those who are underachieving;
- the more able;
- those with special educational needs;
- those who are learning English as an additional language; and
- those experiencing behavioural, emotional and social difficulties;

(l) as relevant to the post in which they are completing induction, effectively take part in and at times lead the work of teaching teams;

(m) as relevant to the post in which they are completing induction, effectively and appropriately deploy, liaise with and manage other adults who support pupils' learning, in and outside the classroom;

(n) secure a good standard of pupil behaviour in the classroom and act to pre-empt and deal with inappropriate behaviour in the context of the behaviour policy of the school.

(Teacher Training Agency, 2002c)

Flexibility within the standards approach

As already mentioned, the *QTS Standards* and the *Induction Standards* consist of outcome statements requiring the teacher to demonstrate certain values, attitudes, knowledge and skills. This approach to QTS and Induction may be considered by some as mechanistic and likely to encourage a checklist view of teaching and training.

While the *QTS Standards* do not set a curriculum, they do set out what is to be assessed and this reflects back to what is to be learned. This is indicated in the earlier quoted words of the then Secretary of State and the Chief Executive of the Teacher Training Agency, that the new Standards and Requirements 'will also help ensure that training tackles issues such as behaviour management and social inclusion well' (Teacher Training Agency, 2002a, p. 1). For example, where one of the Standards is that teachers should demonstrate that 'they understand their responsibilities under the SEN Code of Practice' (ibid., Chapter 2, section 6), it would be odd if initial teacher training did not include the study of the SEN Code. This is not to argue that one should not study the SEN Code but that, where outcome statements are set, it cannot then be claimed that they have absolutely no implications for what is to be learned.

However, the Introduction to the *QTS Standards* suggests that the Standards 'allow providers autonomy in deciding how they will organise their training and respond to individual trainee teachers' needs' (ibid., p. 3). It is open to providers, those seeking QTS and to newly qualified teachers to help ensure a proper balance of different aspects of work leading to QTS and successful induction.

Chapter 1

Defining and distinguishing special educational needs

To meet the Professional Standards for Qualified Teacher Status, teachers must demonstrate that 'They understand how pupils' learning can be effected by their physical, intellectual, linguistic, social, cultural and emotional development' (*QTS Standards*, TTA, 2002a, Chapter 2, section 4).

Regarding the 'complex factors which influence individual pupils' ability to learn', trainees should have 'sufficient understanding of some of these factors to take account of and respond to individual pupil needs, to plan lessons sensitively, and to teach in an inclusive way that recognises pupils have different motivations to learn and that pupils have different needs at different times' (*Handbook of Guidance on QTS Standards and ITT Requirements*, TTA, 2002b, Chapter 2, section 4, scope).

Trainees' knowledge in relation to Standard Chapter 2, section 4 will be indicated in their lesson planning and teaching and the 'strategies they use for differentiation, the approaches they take to organising groups, their selection of resources and their setting of pupil targets will be useful areas of focus'.

In judging trainees' knowledge, assessors may consider the extent to which the trainees work shows evidence 'that perceptual development is a cognitive activity, and that sensory impediments might impair attention and learning' (*Handbook of Guidance on QTS Standards and ITT Requirements*, TTA, 2002b, Chapter 2, section 4, evidence).

Teachers must demonstrate that 'They identify and support more able pupils, those who are working below age-related expectations, those who are failing to achieve their potential in learning and those who experience behavioural, emotional and social difficulties' (*QTS Standards*, TTA, 2002a, Chapter 3, section 2.4).

This chapter analyses the legal definition of SEN distinguishing 'disability', 'difficulty in learning', 'learning difficulty' and 'special educational need'. It outlines the main areas of SEN in line with the *Special Educational Needs Code of Practice* (Department for Education and Skills, 2001a) namely: communication and interaction; cognition and learning; behaviour, emotional and social development; and sensory and/or physical needs. In considering these, reference will be briefly made to the sort of provision from which pupils might benefit as this gives a further indication of the nature of the SEN.

To further illustrate the relationship of disability and SEN, the chapter outlines provisions for SEN and for disability in the Special Educational Needs and Disability Act 2001. I consider the needs of 'looked after' children who have SEN, particularly the responsibilities of social services departments to manage Personal Education Plans for young people. The chapter indicates how the legal definition of SEN helps to distinguish pupils with SEN from pupils for whom English is an additional language and from very able pupils.

The legal definition of special educational needs

The definition of SEN in the Education Act 1996 is: 'a child has special educational needs . . . if he has a learning difficulty which calls for special educational provision to be made for him' (section 312). The Act then defines 'learning difficulty' stating that a child has a learning difficulty if:

'(a) he has a significantly greater difficulty in learning than the majority of children of his age;

(b) he has a disability which either prevents or hinders him from making use of educational facilities of a kind generally provided for children of his age in schools within the area of the local education authority; or

(c) he is under the age of five and is, or would be if special educational provision were not made for him, likely to fall within paragraph (a) and (b) when of, or over that age.'

(section 312 (2))

Learning difficulty, difficulty in learning and disability

It will be seen from the above definition that it is possible to have a learning difficulty but not to have a SEN. This is because the only learning difficulty that constitutes a SEN is one which 'calls for' special educational provision to be made for it.

A child only has a learning difficulty if he has 'a significantly greater difficulty in learning than the majority of children of his age'. This means that a child may have a difficulty in learning which is not significantly greater than that of children of the same age and that therefore would not be considered as a learning difficulty.

A child may have a disability but it may not prevent or hinder him from making use of educational facilities of a kind generally provided for children of his age in schools within the area of the local education authority. Therefore he would not have a learning difficulty.

Consequently, a child may have a disability or a difficulty in learning but may not have a learning difficulty. Similarly, a child may have a learning difficulty but not have a SEN. A child only has SEN when he or she:

- has a 'difficulty in learning' that constitutes a 'learning difficulty' that in turn requires special educational provision, or
- has a 'disability' that constitutes a 'learning difficulty' that in turn requires special educational provision.

A medical condition does not necessarily imply a 'difficulty in learning' or a 'disability' and therefore may not constitute a learning difficulty requiring special educational provision. A medical condition does not therefore necessarily constitute a SEN.

SEN and the *Special Educational Needs Code of Practice*

In the *Special Educational Needs Code of Practice* (Department for Education and Skills, 2001a), the definition of SEN is somewhat elaborated. The *Code* states, on the one hand, that 'there are no hard and fast categories of special educational need', that 'every child is unique' and that 'there is a wide spectrum of special educational need that are frequently inter-related' (Ibid., Chapter 7, section 52). On the other hand, it states that 'there are also specific needs that usually relate to particular types of impairment' (Ibid.) and although 'individual pupils may have needs which span two or more areas', nevertheless, 'needs and requirements can usefully be organised into areas' (Ibid., Chapter 7, section 53). The *Code* then sets out the main areas of SEN as follows:

- communication and interaction (e.g. speech and language delay, impairments or disorders);
- cognition and learning (e.g. moderate, severe and profound and multiple learning difficulties; specific learning difficulties such as dyslexia and dyspraxia);
- behaviour, emotional and social development (e.g. features of emotional and behavioural difficulties, hyperactivity, etc.);
- sensory and/or physical needs (e.g. hearing impairment, visual impairment, physical impairments).

Children whose needs come into these areas are said to require 'flexible teaching arrangements'. It will be apparent that often the areas relate to slower than average progress in some aspect of development, for example, social or emotional or language development. It is assumed in the subsequent sections that the student or newly qualified teacher has a general understanding of physical, cognitive, perceptual, language, social and emotional development as indicated in QTS Standard 2.4 and related *Handbook* guidance (see box above). Special education concerns the learning of pupils where there are difficulties in these areas of development.

Communication and interaction

Among children who, according to the *Code* (DfES, 2001a, Chapter 7, section 55), *will* have communication and interaction difficulties are those with:

- speech and language difficulties, impairments and disorders;
- specific learning difficulties (e.g. dyslexia and dyspraxia);
- hearing impairment;
- autistic spectrum disorder;
- sensory or physical impairment leading to communication and interaction difficulties.

These disorders, difficulties and impairments are in part defined to include communication and interaction difficulties. For example, autistic spectrum disorder (or at least autism) is defined as an impairment of communication and interaction (and other impairments). This is perhaps what the *Code* means when it indicates that 'there are also specific needs that usually relate to particular types of impairment' (Ibid., Chapter 7, section 52).

The *Code* also mentions children who *may* have communication and interaction difficulties. These are children with:

- moderate learning difficulties;
- severe learning difficulties;
- profound learning difficulties.

These 'difficulties' are not exclusively defined according to whether they are associated with communication and interaction difficulties.

Among the educational requirements of pupils with communication and interaction difficulties suggested by the *Code*, some are self-evident. Few would express astonishment in discovering that a pupil with communication and interaction difficulties might require 'help in acquiring, comprehending and using language' or help in using 'different means of communication confidently and competently for a range of purposes' (Ibid., Chapter 7, section 56). Other suggestions include that the pupil may need help in:

- articulation;
- acquiring literacy skills;
- using augmentative and alternative means of communication;

- organising and co-ordinating oral and written language.

Also support may be needed, for example, to 'compensate for the impact of communication difficulty on learning English as an additional language' (Ibid., Chapter 7, section 56).

Cognition and learning

The *Code* considers children who *will* require specific programmes to aid progress in cognition and learning. It is worth asking why anyone should need anything to 'aid' progress and the answer implicit in the *Code* is that some children do not progress as well as others of the same age. This slower progress may be evident, for example, in language development, literacy and numeracy where evidence of this slower progress is lower standards of achievement. Children who are making slower progress than others and who 'require' specific programmes are those who demonstrate features of:

- moderate learning difficulties;
- severe learning difficulties;
- profound learning difficulties;
- specific learning difficulties such as dyslexia.

(Ibid., Chapter 7, section 58)

Again, it is clear that these difficulties imply that progress and achievement are slower than that of other children. It would not make sense to say that special educational provision was to be made because a child had severe learning difficulties and that the evidence for this is that he or she was progressing just as well as everyone else and reaching the same standards of achievement. The very fact that this is not so is what necessitates the 'specific programmes'.

Among those who *may* require specific programmes to aid progress in cognition and learning are children with:

- physical and sensory impairments; or
- autistic spectrum disorder.

The *Code* suggests that pupils with SEN in the area of cognition and learning may require help with such things as:

- acquiring literacy skills;
- organising and co-ordinating spoken and written English to aid cognition;
- processing language, memory and reasoning skills.

(Ibid.)

Behaviour, emotional and social development

The *Code* refers to pupils who 'demonstrate features of' emotional and behavioural difficulties (EBD) and who may be 'disruptive and disturbing'. Other examples of the pupils who are 'demonstrating' features of EBD are those who:

- are withdrawn or isolated;
- are hyperactive and lacking concentration;
- have immature social skills;
- present challenging behaviours arising from other complex special needs.

These children may require help or counselling for certain things. Again, what is required derives unsurprisingly from what it appears pupils do not have. Thus, given that the pupil may have 'immature social skills', he or she may well need 'help with development of social competence'. If the pupil is 'disruptive and disturbing', it follows that they may need 'help in acquiring the skills of positive interaction with peers and adults'. Among other help and support suggested are:

- provision of class and school systems which control or censure negative or difficult behaviours and encourage positive behaviours;
- re-channelling or re-focusing to diminish repetitive and self-injurious behaviours.

Sensory and/or physical needs

The *Code* speaks of a 'wide spectrum of sensory, multi-sensory and physical difficulties' (Ibid., Chapter 7, section 62). Sensory and multi-sensory difficulties include:

- profound and permanent deafness;

- profound and permanent visual impairment;
- lesser levels of loss which may be temporary.

The *Code* refers to physical impairments in terms of their causes (physical, neurological or metabolic), what they might require ('appropriate access to educational facilities and equipment') and what they might lead to ('more complex learning and social needs') (Ibid.).

Among the requirements that the *Code* suggests are:

- appropriate seating, acoustic conditioning and lighting;
- adaptations to the physical environment of the school;
- provision of tactile and kinaesthetic material;
- access to low vision aids.

(Ibid.)

Further information on SEN

A widely used source of further details of SEN and individual differences is the *Special Education Handbook* (Farrell, 2002) which provides information, references, further reading and physical and Internet addresses for a range of areas of SEN and conditions. These include:

Asperger syndrome
attention deficit hyperactivity
   disorder
autism
cerebral palsy
Down's Syndrome
dual sensory impairment
dyslexia
dyspraxia
emotional and behaviour
   difficulties
epilepsy
fragile X syndrome
hearing impairment
mathematics difficulties

moderate learning difficulties
motor impairment
perceptual disorder
physical disability
Prader Willi Syndrome
profound and multiple learning
   difficulties
Rett Syndrome
semantic and pragmatic
   disorders
severe learning difficulties
speech and language
   difficulties
Tourette Syndrome
visual impairment

Special Educational Needs and Disability Act 2001

Background

To further illustrate the relationship of disability to SEN, this section considers the Special Education Needs and Disability Act 2001 (SENDA), which is an important piece of legislation in its own right. The SENDA amends the Disability Discrimination Act 1995 and part 4 of the Education Act 1996 and makes further provision against discrimination on grounds of disability in schools and other educational establishments.

The provisions of the SENDA concerning SEN apply to England and Wales. Provisions relating to the rights of disabled people in education concern England, Wales and Scotland (except the duty to produce an accessibility strategy or plan that does not apply to Scotland).

The SENDA is supplemented by a *Code of Practice* concerning schools (Disability Rights Commission, 2001a) and another *Code of Practice* for the post-16 sector (Disability Rights Commission, 2001b). The Act is in three parts but as part three concerns supplementary matters, we will consider only Parts 1 and 2.

SENDA Part I

Part 1 of the SENDA amends the Education Act 1996 for children with SEN. It strengthens the right of children with SEN to be educated in mainstream schools unless this is incompatible with the wishes of their parents or the provision of efficient education for other children. Also the LEA has to demonstrate that there are no reasonable steps they could take to prevent the incompatibility.

The SENDA requires the LEA to arrange services to provide advice and information for the parents of children with SEN. LEAs must arrange a means of resolving disputes between parents and schools including appointing an independent person to help avoid or resolve disputes. LEAs have to comply within prescribed periods with orders of the Special Educational Needs and Disability Tribunal (SENDIST). Where the LEA decides not to oppose an appeal by a parent to the SENDIST, the appeal is to be treated as having been decided in favour of the appellant.

A school must inform parents where it makes special educational provision for their child. Schools may request a statutory assessment of a pupil's SEN. Revised procedures must be followed by the LEA in making, maintaining and amending statements of SEN, for instance, parents have a right to a meeting with the LEA when it proposes to amend their child's statement.

SENDA Part 2

Part 2 of the SENDA, which has three chapters, concerns disability discrimination in education. Chapter 2 places duties on further and higher education institutions and on LEAs in respect of adult education and youth services provision that they secure. Chapter 3 extends the role of the Disability Rights Commission and allows it to prepare new codes of practice to explain the legislation to education providers, disabled people and others. The Disability Rights Commission may set up an independent conciliation service for disputes arising from the duties of schools under the Act. Its purpose is to promote the settlement of claims without recourse to the SENDIST or other body. Both parent and the 'responsible body' have to agree for disputes to be referred to conciliation.

Chapter 1, which is discussed in the remainder of this section, places duties on LEAs and schools including independent schools and non-maintained special schools in England and Wales. It sets duties on local authorities, independent schools, self-governing schools and grant-aided schools in Scotland.

One key duty is not to treat a disabled pupil less favourably for a reason relating to their disability than someone to whom that reason does not apply, without justification. It is unlawful for a responsible body of a school to discriminate against a disabled child who might become a pupil at the school in relation to its admission arrangements; exclusions or in the education or associated services provided for or offered to pupils at the school.

Three aspects which, taken together, constitute unlawful discrimination are that the less favourable treatment:

- is for a reason that is directly related to the child's disability;
- is less favourable treatment than someone gets if the reason does not apply to them;
- cannot be justified.

Less favourable treatment may be justified if it is the result of a permitted form of selection or is for both a material and substantial reason. A blanket policy does not constitute a material and substantial reason because it takes no account of individual circumstances.

A second key duty is to make reasonable adjustments to admission arrangements, exclusions and in relation to education and related services to ensure that disabled pupils (or prospective pupils) are not substantially disadvantaged in comparison with their non-disabled peers without justification. 'Reasonable adjustments' do not require the responsible body to provide auxiliary aids and services. For schools in the public sector these will be made through the SEN framework. Nor do 'reasonable adjustments' require the responsible body to make physical alterations to the buildings. These are covered by the new planning duties. Generally a school cannot wait until a disabled pupil arrives before making an adjustment. The only justification for not making a reasonable adjustment is that there is a material and substantial reason.

The Act also provides for the possibility that a parent or child may request that the school keep confidential the fact that the child has a disability. In considering what reasonable adjustments to make, a responsible body must keep in mind the extent to which taking a particular step is consistent with maintaining confidentiality, where this has been requested.

The SENDA sets out requirements for England and Wales on LEAs and schools to draw up accessibility strategies (LEAs) and accessibility plans (schools) to improve access to education in schools over time. These strategies and plans have to address the following elements of planned improvements in access for disabled pupils:

- improvements in access to the curriculum;
- physical improvements to increase access to education and associated services;
- improvements in the provision of information in a range of formats for disabled people.

Under the planning duties, governing bodies must include information in their annual reports about the accessibility plan showing how they will increase access for disabled pupils to education at the school.

If parents consider that a responsible body has discriminated against their child, they can claim unlawful discrimination. The SENDIST, which may order any reasonable remedy except financial compensation, will hear such claims relating to:

- fixed-period exclusions from all schools;
- admissions to and permanent exclusions from all schools other than maintained schools and city academies.

Admissions appeals panels or exclusion appeals panels will hear claims of unlawful discrimination regarding a refusal to admit to, and permanent exclusion from, maintained schools and city academies. An admissions appeal is made in compliance with the Code of Practice on Admission Appeals and the panel can order that a pupil be admitted. Exclusion appeals panels can order the pupil's reinstatement.

Looked after children with SEN

In England, within the wider group of children 'in need' are two slightly overlapping groups: (a) children on the child protection register; and (b) children who are 'looked after' by a local authority (Department of Health/Department for Education and Employment/Home Office, 2000).

Under the Children Act 1989, a Care Order may be made placing a child in the care of a local authority and while this is current, the local authority has rights and duties towards the child. These normally include the right to decide where the child is placed. The Court making the order must be satisfied that:

- the child is out of parental control;
- the child is suffering harm (or is likely to suffer harm) from the care currently being given (or likely to be given).

A care order puts the child under the 'care' of the local authority, giving the local authority parental responsibility for the child. A child 'looked after' by a local authority may be the subject of a care order or may be voluntarily accommodated. Day-to-day responsibility may be given to foster parents, guardians or residential social workers.

When a looked after child has SEN, the designated teacher for looked after children works closely with the SEN co-ordinator. Schools should ensure that the child's social worker and, if possible the parents, are involved in the child's education including any special education (Department for Education and Employment/ Department for Health, 2000).

The education of a looked after child may be arranged by social services. The child may also be placed with: a community home with education on the premises; a children's home providing education; or an independent fostering agency providing education.

Where a child is the subject of a care order, or an education supervision order or is accommodated by the local authority, the social services department has to include information on the child's education in the Child Care Plan (CCP). The social services department must review this plan, involving the child in the process. The CCP incorporates a Personal Education Plan setting out the educational arrangements made for the child. This should include information from the child's statement of SEN, Individual Education Plans and any annual review of the statement. LEAs and social service departments may link the review of the CCP with the annual review of the statement of SEN.

Every eligible person who is looked after by a local authority on their 16th birthday (including those with SEN) must have a pathway plan. This integrates with the CCP and Personal Education Plans to aim towards independence. The local authority appoints an adviser who will normally act as the Connexions personal adviser for the young person, devising with them and others the pathway plan and ensuring its implementation (for further information, see Farrell, 2002).

English as an additional language

The legal definition of SEN distinguishes pupils with SEN from pupils for whom English is an additional language. A child for whom English is an additional language may be behind other children of the same age in speaking, understanding and reading and writing English because he or she has had little opportunity to learn the language. In these circumstances the standards of achievement will be lower than the standards of other children. However, the child may not have a 'difficulty in learning' greater than other children of the same age. He or she may progress well in learning English and in other subjects of the National Curriculum. This is not to say of course that they may not need support in learning English perhaps from a specialist teacher. It does, however, mean that the child may not have SEN.

Where a child for whom English is an additional language also happens to have SEN, this may be suggested after careful professional scrutiny of a range of evidence such as that indicating slow progress in:

- learning English;
- other areas of the curriculum including those that are less language based;
- his or her 'main' language.

Very able pupils

The definition of SEN distinguishes pupils with SEN from very able pupils. A pupil who is very able does not by definition have greater difficulty in learning than children of the same age. Nor can it be assumed that a very able pupil has a disability. Therefore it cannot be assumed that the pupil has a learning difficulty or a SEN.

Of course, a pupil may be very able in one area of the curriculum and have a SEN in relation to another, for example, they may be very able in relation to mathematics or music and have SEN relating to literacy. Also a pupil may be very able in curriculum subjects and have an emotional or behavioural difficulty giving rise to SEN.

However, very able pupils do not by virtue of being very able have SEN. Again, this does not imply that they may not benefit from support and specific provision, but this is not special educational provision.

Chapter 2

Inclusion

To meet the Professional Standards for Qualified Teacher Status, teachers must demonstrate that 'They have high expectations of all pupils; respect their social, cultural, linguistic, religious and ethnic backgrounds; and are committed to raising their educational achievement' (*QTS Standards*, TTA, 2002a, Chapter 1, section 1).

'When judging trainees' practice assessors may wish to consider for example: . . . Does the trainee understand that a disabled child, a child with English as an additional language, or a child with a medical condition or diagnosis may not have special educational need (SEN) as defined by law?' (*Handbook of Guidance on QTS Standards and ITT Requirements*, TTA, 2002b, Chapter 1, section 1, evidence).

Teachers must demonstrate that they 'know and understand the Values, Aims and Purposes and the general teaching requirements set out in the *National Curriculum Handbook*' (*QTS Standards*, TTA, 2002a, Chapter 2, section 2). The values and aims set out in the *National Curriculum Handbook* (Department for Education and Employment, 1999a, 1999b) include establishing a curriculum entitlement to pupils 'irrespective of . . . differences in ability and disabilities' (ibid.,

p. 12). The general teaching requirements cover inclusion and providing effective learning opportunities for all pupils (ibid., pp. 30–31).

To meet the Professional Standards for Qualified Teacher Status, teachers must demonstrate that 'They understand how pupils' learning can be affected by their physical, intellectual, linguistic, social, cultural and emotional development' (QTS Standards, TTA, 2002a, Chapter 2, section 4).

Regarding the 'complex factors which influence individual pupils' ability to learn', trainees should have 'sufficient understanding of some of these factors to take account of and respond to individual pupil needs, to plan lessons sensitively, and to teach in an inclusive way that recognises pupils have different motivations to learn and that pupils have different needs at different times' (Handbook of Guidance on QTS Standards and ITT Requirements, TTA, 2002b, Chapter 2, section 4, scope).

Teachers must demonstrate that they 'understand their responsibilities under the SEN Code of Practice, and know how to seek advice from specialists on less common types of special educational needs' (QTS Standards, TTA, 2002a, Chapter 2, section 6).

QTS Standard 2.6 requires trainees 'to be aware of their responsibilities, the legislative requirements relating to SEN and disability, and the rationale for the inclusion of those with special educational needs and disabilities in mainstream education' (Handbook of Guidance on QTS Standards and ITT Requirements, TTA, 2002b, Chapter 2, section 6, scope).

Teachers must demonstrate that they 'have high expectations of pupils and build successful relationships centred on teaching and learning. They establish a purposeful learning environment where diversity is valued and where pupils feel secure and confident' (*QTS Standards*, TTA, 2002a, Chapter 3, section 1, sub-section 1).

'When judging trainees' teaching, assessors may wish to consider, for example: . . . Has the trainee planned to meet diverse needs?' (*Handbook of Guidance on QTS Standards and ITT Requirements*, TTA, 2002b, Chapter 3, section 3, sub-section 1, scope).

This chapter considers definitions of inclusion and the related issue of its remit. It outlines three understandings of inclusion: (1) social inclusion and children who are presently excluded from education; (2) the inclusion of pupils currently in mainstream schools and special schools; and (3) the balance of pupils in mainstream and special schools. Drawing on the *National Curriculum Handbooks* (Department for Education and Employment, 1999a; 1999b), the chapter examines the three principles of inclusion: (1) setting suitable learning challenges; (2) responding to pupils' diverse learning needs; and (3) overcoming potential barriers to learning and assessment for individuals and groups of pupils. Finally, it briefly considers the importance of pupil attainment in inclusion.

Introduction

There is no doubt that thinking about inclusion, as typified in the Salamanca Statement (United Nations Educational, Scientific and Cultural Organisation, 1994), has had an impact on educational thought in recent years. Yet great variation exists in current thinking (Mittler, 2000) and in practice (Ainscow, 1999). Considerable differences exist between different LEAs in how they interpret the word 'inclusion' and how they regard the process (Croll and Moses, 2000; Moore, 2000).

A variety of definitions

Integration is usually taken to assume that a pupil with SEN attends a mainstream school whose systems remain unchanged and in which extra arrangements are made to provide for the pupil's education. Inclusion, where it relates to mainstream schools, encourages the school to review its structures, approaches to teaching, pupil grouping and use of support to enable the school to meet the diverse learning needs of all its pupils.

The Centre for Studies on Inclusive Education (undated) has described inclusion as disabled and non-disabled children and young people learning together in ordinary pre-school provision, schools, colleges and universities, with appropriate networks of support. Their 'Inclusion Charter' (Centre for Studies on Inclusive Education, 1999) with signatories such as the Green Party; the General, Municipal, Boilermakers and Allied Trade Union; thirty-nine Members of Parliament and organisations such as the Chicken Shed Theatre Company, People First and Barnardos, expresses the belief that exclusion of children from the mainstream because of special educational needs is a devaluation and is discriminating.

Writers such as Ballard (1995) and Barton (1995) regard inclusion as a political struggle against exclusive attitudes, approaches and structures of the overall education system. Inclusion is seen as a process through which schools develop responses to value diversity. Similarly, Slee (1996) regards the inclusion policies of local education authorities as seeking to combine the incompatible 'discourses' of social justice with deficit models.

Bailey (1998), from an Australian perspective, regards inclusion as: 'being in an ordinary school with other students, following the same curriculum all the time, in the same classrooms, with the full acceptance of all, and in a way which makes the student feel no different from other students'.

Another perspective emphasises the welcoming and valuing aspect of an 'inclusive' school. All pupils must belong to and be welcomed by and participate in the school and the community. Their range of interests, abilities and attainments are welcomed as an enrichment to the school (e.g. Booth and Ainscow, 1998).

The 1997 'Green Paper' on special education (Department for Education and Employment, 1997), a government consultation document, was concerned with raising standards, increasing inclusion and transferring resources to practical support. Surprisingly, in a document dealing centrally with inclusion, there was no attempt to explicitly define the term. The implicit view that emerges, however, is that inclusion is to do with placing pupils in mainstream schools rather than special schools. The Green Paper sees the peers of pupils with SEN as children in mainstream schools. It refers to 'strong educational as well as social and moral grounds for educating children with SEN with their peers' (Ibid., p. 43). But the Green Paper also envisages the continuation of special schools, stating that: 'parents will continue to have a right to express a preference for a special school' (Ibid., Chapter 4, paragraph 4).

The government document, *Meeting Special Educational Needs: A Programme of Action* (Department for Education and Employment, 1998a), takes a similarly pragmatic approach. It envisages that even if pupils are not placed in mainstream schools they should, where possible, spend as much time as they can in mainstream settings (Ibid., Chapter 3, paragraph 5).

A further view of inclusion which associates it less with particular venues and more with participation is taken by another national body, the Qualifications and Curriculum Authority (Wade, 1999) which sees inclusion as 'securing appropriate opportunities for learning, assessment and qualifications to enable the full and effective participation of all pupils in the process of learning'.

A broad view of diversity and inclusion may be seen in the training booklet connected with OfSTED courses on the inspection of school inclusion (Office for Standards in Education, 2000). This states that educational inclusion is 'more than a concern with one group of pupils such as those who have been or are likely to be excluded from school'. Rather, it is about equal opportunities for all pupils 'whatever their age, gender, ethnicity, attainment or background'. The 'different groups' of pupils concerned include:

- girls and boys;
- minority ethnic and faith groups, Travellers, asylum seekers and refugees;
- pupils who need support to learn English as an additional language;
- pupils with special educational needs;

- gifted and talented pupils;
- children 'looked after' by the local authority;
- other children such as sick children; young carers; those children from families under stress; pregnant schoolgirls and teenage mothers;
- any pupils who are at risk of disaffection and exclusion.

(Ibid., p. 1)

A concern with such a view of inclusion is that by making it so wide, the particular requirements of pupils with SEN (and other particular groups) may be lost. The counter-argument is that children and young people are not just defined by their SEN in isolation but also by other features such as their ethnic group and whether their family is under stress. To recognise this is to provide better for the whole child. While there is some merit in this view, it is also important that the particular knowledge and skills associated with providing for pupils with SEN do not get lost in too broad an approach. This is in line with such developments as the government giving particular consideration to the inclusion of pupils with SEN in such documents as the *Programme of Action* (Department for Education and Employment, 1998a).

Three understandings of inclusion

Among the inter-related ways in which inclusion can be understood are the following:

- the social inclusion and education of children presently excluded from education;
- the inclusion of pupils currently in mainstream schools;
- the balance of pupils in mainstream and special schools.

Social inclusion

Social inclusion is reflected in such documents as *Circular 10/99* (Department for Education and Employment, 1999a) and *Circular 11/99* (Department for Education and Employment, 1999b). *Circular 10/99* notes that children with SEN who develop challenging behaviour are among children at risk of exclusion from school. *Circular 11/99* suggests that LEAs consider legal remedies to compel the attendance of non-attending pupils. The inclusion of some of these children may involve providing education in a pupil support unit or a pupil referral unit.

The inclusion of pupils currently in mainstream schools

Turning to the inclusion of children who are already in mainstream schools, this involves developing a culture in mainstream schools for inclusion, encouraging schools to review their structure, teaching approaches, pupil grouping and use of support so as to respond to the diverse learning needs of all pupils. Teachers would develop opportunities to consider new ways of involving pupils and employ experimentation and reflection. It is important to provide planned access to a broad and balanced curriculum developed from its foundations as a curriculum for all pupils. Teachers will probably have values providing a rationale for inclusive practice, believing that pupils with SEN belong in mainstream classes. As well as a commitment to reviewing performance, there will be a commitment to change. Teachers will draw on various teaching approaches. Collaborative problem solving will help find solutions to challenges arising when teaching a diverse group of pupils.

A document that is used to audit and develop inclusion in a broad sense in mainstream schools is the *Index for Inclusion* (Booth *et al.*, 2000). The document concerns the inclusion of everyone connected with the school, adults as well as children, not just pupils with SEN. It covers three dimensions of schooling: (1) creating inclusive cultures; (2) producing inclusive policies; and (3) evolving inclusive practices. Each dimension is elaborated in a series of indicators which may be used to assess the present situation as well as planning to be, in the Index's terms, more inclusive.

Within the dimension, 'Creating inclusive cultures' one aspect is 'building a community' which includes such indicators as 'everyone is made to feel welcome' and 'staff and students treat one another with respect'. A second aspect is 'establishing inclusive values' which embraces indicators such as 'everyone shares a philosophy for inclusion', and 'staff seek to remove all barriers to learning and participation in the school'.

The dimension, 'producing inclusive policies' includes an aspect, 'developing a school for all' which has indicators such as 'all new staff are helped to settle into the school' and 'the school seeks to admit all students from it locality'. Another aspect, 'organising support for diversity' includes indicators such as '"special needs" policies are inclusion policies' and 'the Code of Practice is used to reduce the barriers to learning and participation of all students'.

Within the dimension 'evolving inclusive practices' is an aspect, 'orchestrating learning' which has indicators such as 'lessons are responsive to student diversity' and 'lessons develop an understanding of difference'. Within the aspect, 'mobilising resources' are indicators such as 'school resources are distributed fairly to support inclusion' and 'student difference is used as a resource for teaching and learning'.

The balance of pupils in mainstream and special schools

Inclusion may relate to increasing the proportion of pupils in mainstream schools in relation to those in specialist provision such as that provided by a special school. This view of inclusion was evident in the SEN Green Paper (Department for Education and Employment, 1997) which stated:

> The ultimate purpose of SEN provision is to enable young people to flourish in adult life. There are therefore strong educational, as well as social and moral, grounds for educating children with SEN with their peers. We aim to increase the level and quality of inclusion within mainstream schools, while protecting and enhancing specialist provision for those who need it.
>
> (Ibid., p. 43)

The impression is sometimes given that fewer and fewer pupils are being educated in special schools. In fact, statistics do not support this. A report published in 1999 indicated that with 242,300 pupils in England with statements of SEN, only 42 per cent were in special schools, a proportion that had reduced over time. However, this change in proportion appears to be due to an increase in the number of pupils with statements of SEN in mainstream schools. The numbers of pupils in special schools had in fact risen over the five years covered by the report to its 'current peak of 93,500 pupils' (Office for Standards in Education, 1999b). A statistical release from the Department for Education and Employment confirmed the picture with more recent figures. Between 1995 and 1999 the total number of pupils in special schools and pupil referral units, including those with and without statements, remained between 97,000 and 99,000 (www.dfee.gov.uk/news/sfr/sfr10htm).

Three principles for inclusion

The National Curriculum document outlines three principles for inclusion: (1) setting suitable learning challenges; (2) responding to pupils' diverse learning needs; and (3) overcoming potential barriers to learning and assessment for individuals and groups of pupils. The following summary picks out the aspects likely to be of particular relevance for pupils with SEN and is not meant to replace reading the relevant passages of the *National Curriculum Handbooks* (Department for Education and Employment/Qualifications and Curriculum Authority (1999a, pp. 30–37 and 1999b, pp. 32–39).

Setting suitable learning challenges

Teachers are encouraged to teach the knowledge, skills and understanding in ways that 'suit their pupils' abilities'. This may mean choosing the knowledge, skills and understanding from earlier stages of the National Curriculum so that 'individual pupils can progress and show what they can achieve'. This may mean that there is insufficient time to teach all aspects of the age-related programmes of study.

For pupils whose attainments fall significantly below expected levels at a particular Key Stage, greater differentiation is necessary. Teachers may need to use the content of the programmes of study as a 'resource' or 'to provide a context' in planning learning, 'appropriate to the age and requirements of the pupils'.

Responding to pupils' diverse learning needs

When planning, teachers should set high expectations and provide opportunities for all pupils to achieve, including pupils with SEN. To help ensure that they meet the full range of pupils' needs, teachers should be aware of the equal opportunities legislation covering race, gender and disability. (Regarding disability, reference is made to the Disability Discrimination Act 1995 but teachers should also be aware of the implications of the Special Educational Needs and Disability Act 2002; for a summary of these and other SEN legislation, see Farrell, 2002.)

Teachers should take 'specific action' to respond to the needs of pupils by doing the following:

- creating effective learning environments;
- securing the motivation and concentration of pupils;
- providing equality of opportunity through teaching approaches;
- using appropriate assessment approaches;
- setting targets for learning.

Overcoming potential barriers to learning and assessment for individuals and groups of pupils

These requirements are seen as applying particularly to the inclusion of pupils with SEN or a disability (and also to pupils for whom English is an additional language).

Regarding pupils with SEN, curriculum planning and assessment 'must take account of the type and extent of the difficulty experienced by the pupil'. In many instances, the action necessary to respond to the requirements of an individual in providing access to the curriculum will involve greater differentiation of tasks and materials. A small number of pupils may 'need access to specialist equipment and approaches or to alternative or adapted activities'. Fewer still will need a statement of SEN.

As appropriate, teachers should work closely with representatives of any other agencies supporting the pupil. Teachers should take specific action to provide access to learning by doing the following:

- providing for pupils who need help with communication, language and literacy;
- planning as necessary to develop pupils' understanding through the use of all available senses and experiences;
- planning for pupils' full participation in learning and in physical and practical activities;
- helping pupils manage their behaviour to participate in learning effectively and safely and at Key Stage 4 to prepare for work;

- helping pupils to manage their emotions and to take part in learning.

Turning to pupils with disabilities (who, as has already been pointed out, do not necessarily have SEN), the document indicates that many such pupils will learn alongside their peers perhaps with the

use of the aids they use in daily life, such as a wheelchair. Teachers must in their planning make sure that disabled pupils are enabled to take part as 'fully and effectively as possible' within National Curriculum and statutory assessment arrangements.

Teachers should take specific action to enable the effective participation of disabled pupils by doing the following:

- planning sufficient time for tasks to be satisfactorily completed;
- planning necessary opportunities for developing skills in practical aspects of the curriculum;
- identifying aspects of the programmes of study and attainment targets that may present difficulties for particular pupils.

Inclusion and pupil attainment

A concern with pupil achievement such as the preoccupation with league tables of school performance is seen as potentially in conflict with the inclusion of diverse learners in the classroom. If school effectiveness is seen only in terms of raising standards of pupil achievement, might this not run counter to the inclusion of more pupils in mainstream schools? As Norwich (2000) has pointed out, it all depends on what one means by 'effectiveness' and 'inclusion'.

Certainly, any approach that purports to move towards inclusion and does not take cognisance of pupil achievement is open to criticism. For example, a criticism of the London Borough of Newham, a local education authority which has sought to become more inclusive, with regard to pupils with SEN and others, was that it had not sufficiently monitored standards of pupil attainment in relation to inclusion. The Office for Standards in Education report which followed an inspection of the LEA stated of the inclusive strategy that:

Overall the LEA knows too little about the impact of the strategy on pupils' attainments. It has managed placements and the provision of support well, but is not in a position to answer the key question: whether attainment and progress of pupils has or has not risen as a result of this strategy (Office for Standards in Education, 1999a, paragraph 143).

Chapter 3

The *Special Educational Needs Code of Practice*

To meet the Professional Standards for Qualified Teacher Status, teachers must demonstrate that 'They are aware of and work within the statutory frameworks relating to teachers' responsibilities' (*QTS Standards*, TTA, 2002a, Chapter 1, section 8).

'[T]rainee teachers need to develop an ability to judge when they may need advice, for example, on matters of child protection or confidentiality, and know how to seek it. This will be particularly important in areas such as the teacher's responsibilities under the *SEN Code of Practice*, or any contribution they may make to formal assessments' (*Handbook of Guidance on QTS Standards and ITT Requirements*, TTA, 2002b, Chapter 1, section 8, scope).

'When judging trainees' practice, assessors will want to draw on observations of trainee teachers' teaching and the reports of school-based tutors for evidence about the professional judgements which trainee teachers make, and the advice they seek, in the course of their practical work with children, colleagues and parents. For example, does the trainee teacher seek advice at an appropriate stage in relation to particular pupils' special educational needs?' (*Handbook of Guidance on QTS Standards and ITT Requirements*, TTA, 2002b, Chapter 1, section 8, evidence).

Teachers must demonstrate that 'They understand their responsibilities under the SEN Code of Practice, and know how to seek advice from specialists on less common types of special educational needs' (*QTS Standards*, TTA, 2002a, Chapter 2, section 6).

QTS Standard 2.6, 'requires trainees to be aware of their responsibilities, the legislative requirements relating to SEN and disability, and the rationale for the inclusion of those with special educational needs and disabilities in mainstream education. This will involve an understanding of the graduated framework of identification, assessment and intervention set out in the SEN Code of Practice; the kinds of provision that might be made through school action, school action plus, and through a statement of special educational needs; and the role of the class or subject teacher within this framework.

In order to seek advice, the teacher will need to be aware of the role of the Special Educational Needs Co-ordinator (SENCO) and how an Individual Education Plan (IEP) is used as a planning and teaching tool' (*Handbook of Guidance on QTS Standards and ITT Requirements*, TTA, 2002b, Chapter 2, section 6, scope).

This chapter examines aspects of the *Special Educational Needs Code of Practice* (Department for Education and Skills, 2001a), hereafter in this chapter referred to as the *Code*. It first sets out the structure and remit of the *Code* principally to help a reader new to the *Code* find their way around the document. The chapter then looks at the principles and critical success factors and at the responsibilities of the early years practitioner and the teacher in the primary and secondary phase in relation to the sort of provision that might be made at different points in the graduated framework. The discussion touches on the role of the SEN Co-ordinator and looks briefly at early intervention and assessment and finally considers some general issues relating to the *Code*. The use of Individual Education Plans (IEPs) as a planning and teaching tool is considered in Chapter 5.

The structure and remit of the *Code*

Following an earlier version introduced in 1994, a revised *Special Educational Needs Code of Practice* (Department for Education and Skills, 2001a) came into effect in January 2002. It gives practical advice to local education authorities (LEAs), maintained schools, early education settings and others on their responsibilities towards all children with SEN.

Among the main changes from the earlier *Code* were that the 2001 *Code* takes account of the SEN provisions of the Special Educational Needs and Disability Act 2001 offering:

- a stronger right for children with SEN to be educated at a mainstream school;
- new duties on LEAs to arrange for the parents of children with SEN to be provided with services offering advice and information and a means of resolving disputes;
- a new duty on schools and relevant nursery education providers to tell parents when they make special educational provision for their child;
- a new right for schools and relevant nursery education providers to request a statutory assessment for a child.

(*Code*, Foreword, paragraph 7)

The *Code* recommends that, in order to help match special educational provision to children's needs, schools and LEAs should adopt a graduated approach. This is achieved through 'School Action' and 'School Action Plus' and in early education settings, through 'Early Years Action' and 'Early Years Action Plus'. A minority of children with the most severe and complex SEN will require statements of SEN.

The *Code* has ten chapters and I will briefly summarise them here. Chapter 1 'Principles and Policies' explains (Chapter 1, section 1) that the purpose of the *Code* is to provide practical guidance to various parties on the discharge of their functions under part 4 of the Education Act 1996. The parties concerned are:

- local education authorities (LEAs);
- the governing bodies of all maintained schools and settings in receipt of government funding to provide early education;
- those who help the above (including health services and social services).

The *Code* (Chapter 1, section 2) sets out guidance on policies and procedures seeking to enable pupils with SEN to reach their full potential, be fully included in their school communities, and make a successful transition to adulthood.

Chapter 2 of the *Code* concerns, 'Working in Partnership with Parents' and Chapter 3 relates to 'Pupil Participation'. Chapter 4, 'Identification, Assessment and Provision in Early Education Settings' identifies providers eligible for government funding as including:

- maintained mainstream and special schools;
- maintained nursery schools;
- independent schools;
- non-maintained special schools;
- local authority day care providers (e.g. day nurseries, family centres);
- other registered day care providers (e.g. pre-schools, play groups, private day nurseries);
- local authority Portage schemes;
- accredited child minders working as part of an approved network.

Early education (foundation stage) concerns children aged 3 to 6 years. The government's 'Early Learning Goals' set out what most children will achieve in various 'areas' (e.g. communication) by the time they enter Year 1 of primary education. The identification of SEN is related to slow progress in the foundation stage. The provider intervenes through 'Early Years Action' and, if progress is still not satisfactory, the SEN co-ordinator may seek advice and support from external agencies ('Early Years Action Plus').

Chapter 5 of the *Code* deals with 'Identification, Assessment and Provision in the Primary Phase' (5 to 11 years) and provides guidance on 'School Action' and 'School Action Plus'. Chapter 6 deals with 'Identification, Assessment and Provision in the Secondary Sector' giving guidance on 'School Action' and 'School Action Plus'.

Chapter 7, 'Statutory Assessment of SEN' has to do with the duties of a LEA under the Education Act 1996, sections 321 and 323, to identify and make a statutory assessment of those children for whom they are responsible who have SEN and who probably need a statement. Broad areas of SEN are identified, and it is indicated that they are not rigid and that there may be a considerable degree of overlap between them. These areas are:

- communication and interaction;
- cognition and learning;
- behaviour, emotional and social development;
- sensory or physical.

Chapter 8, 'Statements of Special Educational Needs', outlines the procedures for making statements and the time scales applicable. Chapter 9 covers the 'Annual Review' of the statement of SEN and the procedures involved. Chapter 10 deals with 'Working in Partnership with Other Agencies'.

Principles and critical success factors

The fundamental principles of the *Code* are that:

- a child with SEN should have their needs met;
- the SEN of children will normally be met in mainstream schools or settings;
- the views of the child should be sought and taken into account;
- parents have a vital role to play in supporting their child's education;
- children with SEN should be offered full access to a broad, balanced and relevant education, including an appropriate curriculum for the foundation stage and the National Curriculum.

(*Code*, Chapter 1, section 5)

The critical success factors are:

- the culture, practice, management and development of resources in school or setting are designed to ensure that **all children's needs are met**;
- LEAs, schools and settings work together to ensure that any child's special educational needs are **identified early**;
- LEAs, schools and settings exploit **best practice** when devising interventions;
- those responsible for special education provision take into account the **wishes of the child** concerned, in the light of their age and understanding;
- special education professionals and **parents** work in **partnership**;
- special education professionals take into account the **views of individual parents** in respect of **their child's particular needs**;
- interventions for each child are **reviewed regularly** to assess their impact, the child's progress and the views of the child, their teachers and their parents;
- there is close co-operation between all the agencies concerned and a **multidisciplinary approach** to the resolution of issues;
- LEAs make assessments within **prescribed time limits**;
- where an LEA determines a child's SEN, statements are **clear and detailed**, made within **prescribed time limits, specify monitoring arrangements** and are **reviewed annually**.

(*Code*, Chapter 1, section 6, bold in original)

The responsibilities of teachers

The *Code* makes it clear that in early education settings, provision for children with SEN is the responsibility of everyone in the setting (Chapter 1, section 29). Similarly, in maintained mainstream schools, provision for pupils with SEN is a matter for the school as a whole and all members of staff have important responsibilities (Chapter 1, section 31). In maintained special schools, again provision for the pupils is a matter for the whole school.

In practical terms, this implies that the new teachers will be careful to assess and monitor the progress of all pupils, being aware when a pupil may have a SEN. This view would be discussed with the SENCO and other colleagues as appropriate.

More specifically, in early years settings, the early education practitioner who works daily with the child or the SENCO may identify a child as having SEN. They then devise interventions that are 'additional to or different from' those usually provided as part of the setting's curriculum and strategies (*Code*, Chapter 4, section 20). The triggers for this intervention, which is known as 'Early Years Action', arise where the parent or the practitioner have concerns about a child who is receiving appropriate education experiences. However, despite these educational experiences, the child:

- makes little or no progress even when teaching approaches are particularly targeted to improve the child's identified area of weakness;
- continues working at levels significantly below those expected for children of a similar age in certain areas;
- presents persistent emotional and/or behavioural difficulties, which are not ameliorated by the behaviour management techniques usually employed in the setting;
- has sensory or physical problems, and continues to make little or no progress despite the provision of personal aids and equipment;
- has communication and/or interaction difficulties, and requires specific individual interventions in order to access learning.

(*Code*, Chapter 4, section 21)

In these circumstances, if the early years practitioner, after consulting parents, considers that the child may need further support to help them progress, they should seek the help of the SENCO.

'Early Years Action Plus' is typified by the involvement of external support services. They may provide advice on IEPs and targets, carry out specialist assessments, or give advice on new or specialist strategies or materials. Triggers for seeking help through School Action Plus could be that in spite of receiving an individualised programme and/or concentrated support, the child:

- continues to make little or no progress in specific areas over a long period;
- continues working at an early years curriculum substantially below that expected of children of a similar age;
- has emotional and/or behavioural difficulties which substantially and regularly interfere with the child's own learning or that of the group, despite having an individualised behaviour management programme;

- has sensory or physical needs and requires additional equipment or regular visits for direct intervention or advice by practitioners from a specialist service;
- has ongoing communication and/or interaction difficulties that impede the development of social relationships and cause substantial barriers to learning.

(Code, Chapter 4, section 31)

In the primary phase, when the class teacher or the SENCO identify a child as having SEN, the class teacher should provide interventions that are 'additional to or different from' those provided as part of the school's usual differentiated curriculum and strategies (Chapter 5, section 43). The triggers for this intervention at 'School Action' could be the concern of a teacher or someone else (supported by evidence) that despite receiving differentiated learning opportunities, the child:

- makes little or no progress even when teaching approaches are particularly targeted in a child's identified area of weakness;
- shows signs of difficulty in developing literacy or mathematics skills which result in poor attainment in some curriculum areas;
- presents persistent emotional and/or behavioural difficulties, which are not ameliorated by the behaviour management techniques usually employed in the school;
- has sensory or physical problems, and continues to make little or no progress despite the provision of specialist equipment;
- has communication and/or interaction difficulties, and continues to make little or no progress despite the provision of a differentiated curriculum.

(Code, Chapter 5, section 44)

If the teacher, in consultation with parents, considers that the child may need further support to help them progress, they should seek the help of the SENCO.

'School Action Plus' is typified by the involvement of external support services. Triggers for seeking help through 'School Action Plus' could be that, in spite of receiving an individualised programme and/or concentrated support under 'School Action', the child:

- continues to make little or no progress in specific areas over a long period;
- continues working at National Curriculum levels substantially below that expected of children of a similar age;
- continues to have difficulty in developing literacy and mathematics skills;
- has emotional and/or behavioural difficulties which substantially and regularly interfere with the child's own learning or that of the class group, despite having an individualised behaviour management programme;
- has sensory or physical needs and requires additional equipment or regular visits for direct intervention or advice by practitioners from a specialist service;
- has ongoing communication and/or interaction difficulties that impede the development of social relationships and cause substantial barriers to learning.

(Code, Chapter 5, section 56)

In the secondary sector the subject teacher or a member of the pastoral team or the SENCO may identify a child as having SEN. The triggers for intervention at 'School Action' (Chapter 6, section 51) and for 'School Action Plus' (Chapter 6, section 64) follow very closely the principles for the primary phase.

When a school or setting requests an LEA to carry out a statutory assessment, it should state the reasons for the request and provide certain evidence. This comprises the views of the parents recorded at 'School Action' or 'School Action Plus' or their early years equivalent; the views of the child in so far as they can be ascertained; and copies of IEPs at 'School Action' or 'School Action Plus' or their early years equivalent. Also needed are evidence of the child's progress; copies of advice from health services and social services where it has been provided; and evidence of the participation and views of professionals with 'relevant specialist knowledge and expertise' beyond the normal competence of the school or setting. Finally, evidence should be provided of the degree to which the school or setting has heeded the advice given by professionals with relevant specialist knowledge (*Code*, Chapter 7, section 13).

The sort of provision that may be necessary for a child requiring or having a statement may include:

- regular and frequent direct teaching by a specialist teacher;
- daily individual support from a learning support assistant;
- a significant piece of equipment such as a closed circuit television or a computer or CD-ROM device with appropriate ancillaries and software;
- the regular involvement of non-educational agencies.

(Code, Chapter 8, section 13)

In any setting, where a child has a statement of SEN, the early years provider or the primary class teacher or the secondary subject teacher continues, with the support of the SENCO, to contribute to provision for the child and to monitor and record progress.

The role of the SEN co-ordinator

As the main source of support and advice regarding pupils with SEN for the new teacher (and other teachers) is the SENCO, it is important to understand their role as outlined in the *Code*. In early education settings the SENCO's responsibilities include advising and supporting other practitioners in the setting. In the primary school, the SENCO's duties may include liaising with and advising fellow teachers and contributing to the in-service training of staff.

In the secondary school responsibilities are similar to those in the primary school except that the SENCO may be responsible for other duties such as liaising with external agencies including the LEA's support and educational psychology services, the Connexions personal adviser, health and social services, and voluntary bodies. The reader should consult the *Code* where a fuller list of responsibilities of the SENCO is given with respect to early education settings (Chapter 4, sections 15–16), primary schools (Chapter 5, section 32) and secondary schools (Chapter 6, section 35).

The *National Standards for Special Educational Needs Co-ordinators* (Teacher Training Agency, 1998) regard the SENCO as being responsible for four areas of SEN co-ordination:

- the strategic direction and development of SEN in the school;
- teaching and learning;
- leading and managing staff;
- the efficient and effective deployment of staff and resources.

The SENCO is often the new teacher's first point of contact with other specialists involved in SEN. The roles of some of these specialists are described in Chapter 12.

Early intervention and the use of assessment

Early intervention cannot always mean the assessment of SEN when the child is very young, for SEN may arise when a child is in adolescence because of accidental injury or owing to family breakdown. Early intervention therefore really means prompt intervention once SEN are recognised.

Routine school assessments that apply to all pupils will often indicate that a child has greater difficulties in learning than children of the same age or whether the child has a disability that is preventing or hindering them from making use of the usual educational facilities. Assessments that are more detailed may then follow to examine whether the disability or difficulty in learning constitutes a learning difficulty that might require special educational provision.

Baseline assessment is important in establishing the child's strengths and weakness and aspects of the learning environment that may be creating difficulties. This also forms a basis from which to judge the effectiveness of further interventions.

Chapter 4

Equal opportunities and local SEN policy

To meet the minimum requirements of the Professional Standards for Qualified Teacher Status, teachers must demonstrate that 'They recognise and respond effectively to equal opportunities issues as they arise in the classroom, including by challenging stereotyped views, bullying or harassment, following relevant policies and procedures' (*QTS Standards*, TTA, 2002a, Chapter 3, section 3, sub-section 14).

'When judging trainees' teaching, assessors might consider . . . Does the trainee ensure the fullest participation of pupils with disabilities or medical needs?' (*Handbook of Guidance on QTS Standards and ITT Requirements*, TTA, 2002b, Chapter 3, section 3, sub-section 14).

This chapter, viewing SEN in the light of equal opportunities, first looks at the terms 'equal opportunities' and 'equity'. It next considers how equal opportunities issues relating to SEN may arise in the classroom in relation to stereotyped views. The chapter then focuses on local policy, concentrating on LEA policy as well as school SEN policy and related documents.

Equal opportunities and equity

The expression 'equal opportunities' is sometimes used in relation to groups identified according to SEN, race, gender, nationality,

religion, social class, sexual orientation or some other characteristic.
It can mean:

- equality of access;
- equivalent experience;
- overcoming limitations; or
- equality of outcome.

(Farrell *et al.*, 1995, p. 81)

Equality of access involves ensuring that people have the same
available opportunities. With SEN this may relate to a pupil with
visual impairment being provided with instruction in Braille to aid
access to both learning and to a broad and balanced school
curriculum.

'Equivalent experience' is intended to enable each person to
fulfil his or her potential. However, a person's potential cannot be
securely known and equivalence embodies a value judgement on
which it might be difficult to agree. It would not be easy to agree
the equivalent experience for a pupil with profound learning difficulties and a pupil without learning difficulties studying, say, a
course in history that did not risk being seen as cosmetic.

Overcoming limitations may relate to limited experiences of
learning because of earlier experiences of stereotyping. This overlaps with the notion of barriers to learning. Low expectations for
a pupil with SEN relating to stereotyping may have led to experiences being unnecessarily limited, for example, the pupil may not
have been engaged in sufficiently challenging activities.

Equality of outcome refers to ensuring that different groups
reach equal levels of achievement compared with other groups.
For example, pupils with emotional and behavioural difficulties
may be expected to achieve at similar levels to pupils without emotional and behavioural difficulties with comparable levels of prior
learning.

Equality of opportunity in a school is reflected in features
such as:

- school aims and objectives;
- policies;
- staffing structures;
- curricular plans and organisation;
- pupil groupings;

- pupil records;
- relationships within the school.

(Farrell, 1999, p. 74)

Related to equal opportunities is the notion of 'discrimination' which implies less favourable treatment that cannot be justified and that is based on a specified difference. In SEN, for example, the Special Education Needs and Disability Act 2001 sets out what constitutes disability discrimination in education. Discrimination is taken to occur if without justification a 'responsible body' such as a school 'for a reason which relates to his disability' treats a disabled pupil 'less favourably than it treats or would treat others to whom that reason does not apply'. If the responsible body does treat a disabled pupil in such a way, it must show that the treatment is justified. Equity relates to fairness and more specifically to applying the principles of justice to correct the law or to supplement it.

Within this context, policy and provision for pupils with SEN may be seen as a way of helping ensure equality of access and overcoming limitations. Any policy taking this perspective would set out how access was to be aided and how it was proposed that any limitations were to be overcome.

Equal opportunities issues relating to SEN in the classroom and stereotyped views

If the teacher aims to offer equality of opportunity and seeks to overcome limitations, it is helpful to consider any stereotyped views that may hinder this, whether those views come from the teacher, the pupil with SEN, other pupils or elsewhere.

A stereotyped view may be seen as one which generalises from a group to an individual without any evidence as to whether the general view applies to the individual. If the generalisation about the group is incorrect in any way, it is clearly unreasonable to infer from this that the generalisation applies to members of that group. However, even if an assumption is correct in the general sense, it does not follow that it is appropriate to assume that members of the group conform to what may be typical of the group.

For example, it may be correct that girls perform better in mathematics than boys in General Certificate of Secondary Education examinations in England in the early years of the millennium.

But to assume that a particular boy will perform at a lower level than a particular girl would be to inappropriately carry general truths over to particular cases without evidence (this is leaving aside the possibility that the general trends may change). Such an assumption stereotypes the individual boy and may lead to lower expectations of performance than would be justified.

Where such assumptions relate to pupils with SEN, it is important to challenge them. The way such assumptions may inter-relate with assumptions to do with other aspects of individuality such as gender, ethnicity, social background and age has also to be considered. A practical way of examining these relationships is to consider the cohort of pupils with SEN and examine their achieve-ment and progress in terms of different sub-groups.

For example, if pupils with SEN are considered in terms of ethnicity, do pupils with SEN from ethnic minority backgrounds reach similar levels of achievement and make similar progress to pupils with SEN who are not from an ethnic minority? If not, why not? An examination of access to within school and out of school activities, staff role models, the interest level of text books, com-puter software and other resources might indicate possible reasons. Underlying these may be stereotypical views of how pupils from different ethnic groups learn which may not be justified. Steps may then be taken to address the disparity (Farrell, 2001).

LEA policy on special educational needs

An important aspect of the context in which the new teacher works is that of the LEA. The role of the modern LEA in school education is changing (Department for Education and Employ-ment, 2000c). Authorities are expected to give a full account to schools and local council taxpayers of the money delivered. This includes money provided through spending assessment and through specific grants. There will also be an indication of the proportions funded through government and through locally raised finance and comparisons with the previous year. Among the essential functions that individual schools are not expected to carry out but which involve LEAs is 'taking decisions, in consultation with schools, about the distribution of the schools' budget to take account of schools' differing needs' (Department for Education and Employment, 2000c, p. 7, paragraph 11). Strategically, the LEA will maintain a capacity to develop policy, set priorities, allocate resources, and draw up plans for delivery in relation to the Authority's central functions.

It is important that LEAs identify and disseminate good practice. LEAs will also work within a more open market for school services. This may include offering an independent 'brokerage' service, putting schools in contact with a range of suppliers to achieve the best value from their delegated budgets (Ibid., p. 13, paragraph 24).

The role of the LEA in relation to schools can be summarised under the four 'fair funding' headings: (1) special educational needs; (2) access (to school places); (3) school improvement; and (4) strategic management.

One of the key roles of an LEA is in statutory functions particularly with regard to SEN. Already a range of voluntary and private sector groups are working with LEAs. Regional collaboration projects aim to co-ordinate provision for pupils with low incidence SEN.

The LEA remit includes 'ensuring that the individual needs of children are quickly and accurately identified and matched by appropriate provision' (Ibid., p. 7, paragraph 13a). It also includes running an education psychology service and support teaching services, linking with social and health services and planning the use of resources 'so that individual children can benefit from co-ordinated provision through their school' (Ibid., p. 8, paragraph 13a). An overlapping area is that of educating excluded pupils with behavioural difficulties.

The LEA policy relating to SEN may have been developed by a group of people representing a range of interests and should have been the subject of wide consultation. The layout and structure of a policy on SEN will reflect its remit and therefore the remit of the policy should be clear. It may focus on SEN and relate to other policies including those on other aspects of inclusion such as those for ethnic minority pupils, pupils looked after by the local authority, refugees and asylum seekers and others. Or it could be comprehensive and cover all the areas of inclusion.

The policy should give due weight to teaching and learning. The SEN policy may have several sections. One will be a brief introductory statement of intent perhaps called a 'policy statement'. The policy statement would set the local policy in the context of national developments and trends as well as succinctly stating the point of the policy. Another section might set out the underlying principles reflecting national as well as local issues and would seek to define key terms such as 'inclusion', 'equality of opportunity' and 'accountability'.

There may be a succinct outline of the results of a 'best value' audit indicating how the LEA is performing compared with similar LEAs. This might cover issues such as the percentage of pupils identified as having SEN, with and without statements and the balance of pupils with statements educated in special schools, units in mainstream schools, and in mainstream classrooms. It may be based on data from statistically similar LEAs – so-called statistical neighbours. This information can be helpful but needs to be treated with caution. For example, the sample size may be very small in certain comparisons such as that of the proportion of pupils moving between special and mainstream schools. The best value audit would be one of the sources of data that would help determine financial approaches underpinning the policy.

Aims and objectives may form other sections of the SEN policy. The aims might be such things as 'to ensure that all individual pupils make progress in their learning and development, enabling them to reach a greater level of achievement and personal and social development' and 'to ensure that schools continue to improve standards of teaching and learning'.

Main objectives might concern the work of schools and others at different 'levels' of SEN. This would be expressed in terms of the intervention that a school or early years setting might make (school and early years action), the level at which outside intervention is deemed appropriate (action plus) and the level at which a statement is necessary. The objectives may be such issues as, 'to work with schools and others to develop effective provision for *school and early years action* and *action plus* and pupils with statements of SEN'. Another objective might be 'to ensure the effective use of data on SEN and to develop a more systematic approach to the monitoring of SEN including sharing information with schools and cost effectiveness'. These might be followed by a list of actions to be taken by participants in the policy to achieve its aims expressed simply and clearly.

The policy should set out specific targets such as 'improve the time taken to produce provisional statements of SEN by increasing the percentage completed in the recommended number of weeks from 50% to 95% in one year'. More detailed action plans may have been developed separately, specifying exactly how each target will be achieved, including the strategies to be adopted to reach the targets.

Links should be carefully tracked from the SEN policy to other policies and vice versa, articulating clear intentions to integrate policy actions as appropriate. For instance, the SEN policy may state an intention to extend the inclusion of pupils with SEN (including those with emotional, behavioural and social difficulties) through various means, including developing the ability of mainstream schools to provide for a wider range of pupils than they do presently. The policy on behaviour (linked to the behaviour development plan) would then specify the particular ways in which the LEA will help develop the ability of schools to provide for pupils with difficult behaviour.

Another policy may concern pupils from ethnic minorities. Both this policy and the SEN policy would agree the approach and provision for pupils from ethnic minorities who have SEN. For example, the policies may include a commitment to analyse data on the identification of different SEN. This would indicate whether the representation of pupils with ethnic minorities reflected the proportion of such pupils in the schools or whether pupils from ethnic minorities appeared to be under- of over-represented in different areas of SEN.

Planning of course relates to policy and the most central overall LEA plan is the Education Development Plan (EDP) which LEAs have to submit to the Department for Education and Skills (DfES). The EDP has sections referring to SEN and the main thrust of these should be elaborated in the SEN policy and presented in more detail in SEN action plans.

Among other plans required by the DfES are an early years development plan, and a behaviour development plan. There may also be plans covering the achievement of pupils from ethnic minority backgrounds and others. Plans developed by the Health Services include the Child Care Plan and the Children Strategy Group Plan. The Social Services have various plans too, including the Assessment Plan.

The new teacher need not consult all of these plans, of course, although they may be referred to from time to time in local education authority policies provided in service education and training. It may be informative to look through the LEA policy for SEN.

School SEN policy

Policy is not just a matter of having the correct documentation but also ensuring that the policy was developed in such a way as to guarantee that those following it understand and endorse it. Given the numerous written policies that a school has to have, this represents a considerable investment of time and effort on the part of the whole school community and beyond. However, the work and thought that go into developing and refining policies are as important as the written policy itself.

It is therefore likely that if there has been wide discussion and consultation in the development and later refinement of the policy, it will be more effective. Staff will tend to subscribe to it more readily, understand it more fully and use it more productively. Parents and others will tend to support it.

Schools and certain other educational settings have to have a written SEN policy. These settings are:

- those that receive government funding for early education;
- maintained nursery schools;
- community, foundation and voluntary schools;
- community and foundation special schools;
- City Academies;
- City Technology Colleges;
- City Colleges for Technology of the Arts.

The SEN policy must contain certain information as set out in *Statutory Instrument 2506*, the *Education (Special Educational Needs) (Information) Regulations 1999* which form an appendix to the *Special Educational Needs Code of Practice* (Department for Education and Skills, 2001a). SEN policies in early education settings and City Academies must contain information as set out in the conditions of the grant. Also, local education authorities (LEAs) must ensure that pupil referral units (for which the LEA form a management group) have suitable SEN policies.

Governing bodies of all maintained mainstream schools must publish information on the schools' SEN policy and report on the policy. The governing body must at least annually 'consider and report on' their school policies and on the effectiveness of the school's work for pupils with SEN. The governing body's annual report must include information on the implementation of the governing body's policy on pupils with SEN and any changes to the policy in the previous year.

The information required by *Statutory Instrument No. 2506* is set out in three schedules. Schedule 1 deals with information from maintained schools, schedule 2 with maintained special schools, and schedule 3 with special schools in hospitals. Taking schedule 1 as an example, the information provided in the SEN policy covers:

- basic information about the school's special educational provision;
- information about the school policies for the identification, assessment and provision for all pupils with SEN;
- information about the school's staffing policies and partnership with bodies beyond the school.

Basic information about the school's special educational provision includes the objectives of the governing body in making provision for pupils with SEN and 'a description of how the governing body's SEN policy will contribute towards meeting those objectives'. This objective needs to be given particular thought by the school because on it rests the whole point of making provision for pupils with SEN at all. Ensuring that the policy assists those objectives may seem basic but is also crucial.

Information about the school policies for the identification, assessment and provision for all pupils with SEN include 'how resources are allocated to and amongst pupils with SEN'. Another item is 'how the governing body will evaluate the success of the education which is provided at the school to pupils with SEN'. Resources refer not only to physical learning resources but also to the money received by the school relating to SEN and what is done with it. The governing body's evaluation of success is a central part of the policy and if the aims of the policy are sufficiently challenging, this will feed into the improvement of provision in subsequent years.

The information about the school's staffing policies and partnership with bodies beyond the school covers such items as 'the role played by the parents of pupils with SEN'. Such objectives come to mean different things as other regulations and guidance develop the role of parents.

Annual reports and school prospectuses

Related to this, governors' annual reports and school prospectuses for primary and secondary schools must include specified information on SEN (Department for Education and Skills, 2000a; 2000b). If it is assumed that the annual report and the prospectus are published separately, both must include:

- a summary of the governing body's policy on children with SEN;
- any significant changes to that policy since the previous governors' annual report;
- a statement on the success in implementing the governing body's SEN policy in the last year.

The annual report only has to include:

- a description of the admission arrangements for pupils with disabilities;
- details of steps taken to prevent pupils with disabilities from being treated less favourably than other pupils;
- details of existing facilities provided to assist access to the school by pupils with disabilities;
- the accessibility plan setting out the school's future policies for increasing disability access to the school.

Chapter 5

Raising educational achievement and the use of Individual Education Plans

To meet the Professional Standards for Qualified Teacher Status, teachers must demonstrate that 'They have high expectations of pupils; respect their social, cultural, linguistic, religious and ethnic backgrounds; and are committed to raising their educational achievement' (*QTS Standards*, TTA, 2002a, Chapter 1, section 1).

Teachers must demonstrate that 'They understand their responsibilities under the SEN Code of Practice, and know how to seek advice from specialists on less common types of special educational needs' (*QTS Standards*, TTA, 2002a, Chapter 2, section 6).

In line with *QTS Standard* 2.6, 'In order to seek advice, the teacher will need to be aware of the role of the Special Educational Needs Co-ordinator (SENCO) and how an Individual Education Plan (IEP) is used as a planning and teaching tool . . . Trainees will not be expected to have the same level of expertise as experienced teachers of the SENCO, or to draw up an IEP independently' (*Handbook of Guidance on QTS Standards and ITT Requirements*, TTA, 2002b, Chapter 2, section 6, scope).

Teachers should demonstrate that 'As relevant to the age group they are trained to teach, they are able to plan opportunities for pupils to learn in out-of-school contexts, such as school visits, museums, theatres, field-work and employment-based settings with the help of other staff where appropriate' (*QTS Standards*, TTA, 2002a, Chapter 3, section 1, sub-section 5).

'They differentiate their teaching to meet the needs of pupils, including the more able and those with special educational needs. They may have guidance from an experienced teacher where appropriate' (*QTS Standards*, TTA, 2002a, Chapter 3, section 3, sub-section 4).

Evidence relevant to meeting *QTS Standard* (Chapter 3, section 3, sub-section 4) includes: 'If trainees work in a school that has a unit for pupils with impaired vision or hearing, they might present evidence on how they differentiate their teaching to meet the needs of one or more such pupils. Records of pupils' progress provide trainees with the opportunity to explain how their teaching takes account of the Individual Education Plans of pupils with special educational needs' (*Handbook of Guidance on QTS Standards and ITT Requirements*, TTA, 2002b, p. 45).

To meet the Induction Standards, NQTs should, by the end of the induction period, 'plan effectively, where applicable, to meet the needs of pupils with special educational needs, with or without statements, and in consultation with the SENCO contribute to the preparation, implementation, monitoring and review of Individual Education Plans or their equivalent' (*Induction Standards* (e), TTA, 2002c).

This chapter considers teacher expectations and how the standards of educational achievement and educational attainment of pupils with SEN can be improved. Particular attention is paid to Individual Education Plans (IEPs). This chapter also considers how extra-curricular and out-of-school activities might be planned to include pupils with SEN.

Standards of pupil achievement

Raising the 'educational achievement' (*QTS Standards*, Chapter 1, section 1) of pupils is indicated by raising the levels of pupil achievement. This may be understood in a broad sense as including such achievements as literacy, numeracy and other curriculum areas but also very importantly, personal, social and emotional development.

Expectations and standards

Having high expectations of pupils with SEN and improving educational standards are related. On the one hand, it is necessary to identify pupils with SEN and to recognise areas of SEN that may suggest common approaches. For example, a primary pupil may have been identified as having severe learning difficulties (SLD). The teacher may consider that a suitable approach may be one broadly drawing on a developmental curriculum below level 1 of the National Curriculum and leading into level 1 of the National Curriculum and higher as appropriate. Continuing progress and standards of pupil attainment may be assessed using such assessments as the Performance Descriptors (Department for Education and Employment, 2001a). On the other hand, it is necessary to avoid assumptions about children as a group (those with severe learning difficulties) unduly suppressing the expectations of individual pupils. For instance, the assessment of severe learning difficulties might be partially owing to deprivation and lack of opportunities for learning and development. To the degree that this is so, then progress might be better than for many other pupils with SLD. To assume that there are no individual differences may be to set expectations too low.

This is difficult professional judgement. Not to assume some common features of pupils with severe learning difficulties is to start from scratch with every pupil and this would negate much of the professional expertise accumulated by specialist teachers and others concerning an appropriate curriculum, assessment and teaching approaches. But not to respond sufficiently to individual pupils and their development may lead to expectations being too low. If expectations are too high, they are likely to be unrealistic, if too low, they may be constraining.

Similar points could be made regarding expectations of the behaviour of pupils with emotional, social and behavioural difficulties or expectations of those with hearing impairments, and so on. Low expectations can lead in extreme instances to the pupils' SEN being the 'reason' for their slow progress and low standards in a depressing (in both senses of the word) circular argument. In this scenario, the reason why the standard of literacy of a group of pupils is low is that 'they have SEN'. SEN may be indicated for these pupils largely by the low literacy scores. Therefore the reason for the low levels of literacy is that the children in this cohort cannot read very well! Perhaps the underlying reason for such a circular argument is that there can be too much emphasis on 'meeting needs' (a nebulous obscure term often concealing value judgements of what the teacher or others consider is good for the child). Perhaps there should be less emphasis on meeting needs and more on raising standards of pupil achievement.

Individual Education Plans

While Individual Education Plans (IEPs) are of course planning documents, they are also documents that inform teaching and contribute to monitoring, recording and reporting a pupil's progress and attainment. They set out approaches that are adopted over and above the differentiation of teaching used to respond to the learning needs of pupils with SEN.

A useful overview of the use of Individual Education Plans (IEPs) is given in the *SEN Toolkit* (Department for Education and Skills, 2001d). An IEP is seen as a tool for planning teaching and reviewing which should 'underpin' the process of planning intervention for a pupil with SEN. The plan should set out the content, methods and frequency of knowledge, understanding and skills to be taught through activities that are additional to and different from those provided by the differentiated curriculum. It is not a document solely for the SEN Co-ordinator but a 'working document for all teaching staff'. The IEP concerns the differentiated steps and teaching requirements needed to help the pupil to reach specified targets. IEPs should be agreed where possible with the involvement of the parents and the pupil concerned.

The *SEN Toolkit* envisages that an IEP will be used for pupils requiring support through 'Early Years Action', 'Early Years Action Plus', 'School Action', 'School Action Plus' and Statements of SEN. It is emphasised that IEPs record only short-term targets and strategies that are different from or additional to those for the rest of the class.

IEPs should include up to three or four individual targets relating to communication, literacy, mathematics and aspects of behaviour of physical skills. In line with guidance in the *Special Educational Needs Code of Practice* (Department for Education and Skills, 2001a), the IEPs should include information about:

- prioritised short-term targets;
- teaching strategies to be used;
- provision to be put in place;
- when the plan is to be reviewed;
- success criteria;
- outcomes.

Generally, targets should be SMART that is, specific, measurable, achievable, relevant and time bound.

The *SEN Toolkit* also suggests that group education plans may be used, for example, where a school arranges for a group of pupils with 'similar needs' and one or more shared targets to be taught together. However, where pupils have targets and strategies that are additional to the group education plan, these would be recorded on an IEP.

The *SEN Toolkit* (Department for Education and Skills, 2001d, paragraph 28) perhaps rather optimistically states that 'By integrating IEPs within the general organisation of planning, assessment, recording and reporting, the management of IEPs will be less onerous.' A more realistic if minor way of reducing the paperwork burden is the suggestion that in monitoring IEPs, if progress remains adequate after two reviews, the period between reviews may be increased (Ibid., paragraph 41).

The continuing concern with the bureaucracy of IEPs is reflected, to take only one illustration, in the findings of a survey of secondary school SEN Co-ordinators in Cornwall (Lingard,

2001). Asked if IEPs often describe the help that would be in place anyway in the school, twenty-one out of twenty-five respondents said they did. When asked if children at their school would learn just as effectively without IEPs, twenty out of twenty-seven respondents believed they would. There was massive agreement (twenty-four out of twenty-six) that the time spent writing and administering IEPs would be better spent on direct pupil support. Review meetings were thought to be mainly attended by parents who would support their children anyway (twenty-seven of thirty-six respondents). A related lack of confidence concerned target setting in which fifteen of twenty-six respondents believed that target setting was problematic because it is extremely difficult to predict how much progress a child will make.

This last point illustrates that a difficulty with IEPs if one is striving to raise educational standards for pupils with SEN is that the targets set in them may be too low and unchallenging. Teachers and others may seek to set realistic but challenging targets. However, these have not always in the past had the credibility of similar targets set for pupils who do not have SEN and which are related to expectations of pupils at the end of Key Stages in National Curriculum tests.

The difficulty in establishing the credibility of IEP targets have rendered judgements about the progress of pupils in schools inspected by the Office for Standards in Education (OfSTED) inspectors subjective. In inspections, judgements on the progress of pupils with SEN have been essentially based on evidence that targets set by the school in IEPs have been reached in the time specified on the IEP. It has not been possible to make judgements about progress in relation to expectations of standards of pupil achievement. So-called judgements of standards of pupils with SEN have tended to be descriptions of what the pupils have been observed doing.

In special schools the picture was equally confused. An OfSTED report (Office for Standards in Education, 1999) observed that in the 'great majority' of special schools it was 'inappropriate' to try to judge pupils' attainments against national norms. Before 1997, standards used to be judged on the basis of pupils' 'achievement' and this was determined by pupils' attainment in relation to their 'capability', although how the capability of pupils was to be judged was not clear. In 1996/7 a new Framework for Inspection was introduced. This replaced the earlier judgements about standards with the idea that pupil progress was the key indicator of standards. The report acknowledged that the change made the analysis of trends 'problematic' but did not appear to recognise the fundamental problem of trying to assess standards or progress without reference to external uniform criteria.

Fortunately this situation is improving, moving more towards that of all pupils. In turn, this will offer the opportunity to improve the quality and usefulness of IEPs. For example, for pupils with learning difficulties, curriculum guidance has been developed linked to performance descriptors to help assess standards and progress (Department for Education and Employment/ Qualifications and Curriculum Authority, 2001). As these become increasingly embedded in routine school assessments, a clearer indication should emerge of the standards of all pupils including those with SEN.

Admittedly, the performance descriptors will be based on teacher assessment with its own attendant worries about subjectivity while indicators of standards for pupils without SEN tend to involve standard assessment tests which (despite any limitations they may have) offer better comparability. But with good training for the teachers using the performance descriptors and with an effective system of moderating the teacher judgements in each school, an approach using performance descriptors has the potential to be an improvement on the previous use of IEP targets.

The use of agreed performance descriptors should enable benchmarking and target setting to be carried out for cohorts of pupils with SEN in a similar way to that used for other pupils. Once it is more established what standards are evident in schools with similar cohorts of pupils with SEN, and what can therefore be reasonably expected, then this information will be able to be used to reflect back on the function and quality of IEPs. They can then have the potential to draw on the broader targets that have been set for the whole cohort of pupils in the school with SEN. Individual targets can then be informed by this information.

Whole school and whole cohort targets are set using not just predictions of the progress and standards expected of pupils but with an added element to push achievement still higher than that predicted. Because of this there is an extra challenge built into the setting of individual targets on IEPs as these targets must contribute to the whole cohort targets.

This cycle has the potential, if used professionally, to raise the credibility of IEPs and their targets from being at worst *ad hoc* and flaccid to being challenging and related to aspirations for the realistic progress of the wider cohort of pupils with SEN.

The use of IEP information is limited in some schools because of a tendency to insufficiently recognise the enormously important contribution of all teachers in improving the standards and progress of pupils with SEN. At worst a school may see the individual work of a learning support assistant, a support teacher or the SEN Co-ordinator as the main or even the sole contributor to the raising standards of pupils with SEN. As the bulk of a pupil's time in school is usually spent with non-specialist teachers, a vital contribution to raising the standards of pupils with SEN comes from them. Consequently it is important that *all* teachers have information drawn from IEPs that is immediately accessible, is used in planning lessons and has an impact on the provision for the pupils with SEN.

In some schools each teacher has in each lesson a note of the SEN of each child with SEN and a brief reminder of the provision that follows from this. For example, 'general learning difficulty – ensure instructions understood, may need extra time.' 'Hearing impairment – ensure you are facing the child and child should sit near front of class.' Of course, such simple *aide-mémoires* may be drawn from more detailed IEPs but particularly in secondary schools where a teacher may see fifty or more pupils with SEN each week, such cribs are an aid to the sort of extra differentiation necessary within the whole class.

The focus on standards and progress should refine the information on IEPs and reduce it. Much information on IEPs and other records that is descriptive and is not used can often be safely discarded.

Particular issues arise when preparing and monitoring IEPs for pupils with emotional, social and behavioural difficulties. While the targets will need to be few and will have to be prioritised, it is likely to be helpful if they include behaviour and relationships as well as more academic targets. This may achieve two goals. First, it may help the SENCO and all staff monitor the effectiveness of the strategies that are being used to encourage appropriate behaviour and discourage inappropriate conduct. Second, it may help staff to keep an equal focus on raising standards of achievement in school subjects, particularly in literacy, communication, and mathematics. This is likely to contribute to improved self-esteem and a sense of achievement for the pupil which may help improve behaviour. Also, having academic targets will help ensure that members of staff do not focus on behaviour and emotional and social development at the expense of 'academic' progress.

Planning out-of-school learning opportunities to include pupils with SEN

In the QTS Standards, teachers must be able 'to plan opportunities for pupils to learn in out-of-school contexts, such as school visits, museums, theatres, field-work and employment-based settings with the help of other staff where appropriate' (*QTS Standards*, Teacher Training Agency, 2002a, Chapter 3, section 1, sub-section 5).

The principles involved in different forms of out-of-school working are similar and may be illustrated by taking the example of a theatre visit to see a play. The key terms are planning and learning. As with school-based lessons and activities, the learning outcomes should be as clear for a pupil with SEN as for any other pupil. It should be evident at the end of the visit that the learning outcome has been achieved. For example, the learning outcome for a pupil who has emotional and behavioural difficulties making concentration and relationships difficult may be:

- to give a spoken account of the action/plot of the play on returning to school;
- to sit throughout the play without disturbing others.

The planning will be based on a close knowledge of the pupil and an understanding of the environment in which the play will take place (for example, in an indoor or outdoor theatre). To support the pupil giving an account of the play, preparation work in school may involve familiarising the pupil with the main characters and the setting of the play and an indication of the theme (murder, romance). This will help structure the experience and give the pupil more opportunity to focus on the action.

To help the pupil reach the second learning objective, preparation is again the key. It may involve considering the proposed seating arrangements carefully, determining with the pupil whether she or he will sit with an adult or other pupils and, if with other pupils, with whom. Planning may involve arriving at the theatre just in time for the play so that there is no excessive time waiting in the theatre. It may suggest sitting at the end of a row if the pupil is likely to need to go out from time to time. The balance is between helping ensure that the pupil learns from the experience and not having expectations that are too low. The involvement of the pupil in the planning will be important so that the reasons for it are clearly understood.

Chapter 6

Literacy and numeracy

To meet the Professional Standards for Qualified Teacher Status, teachers must demonstrate that 'for *reception* children [they know and understand] the frameworks, methods and expectations set out in the National Numeracy and Literacy Strategies' (*QTS Standards*, TTA, 2002a, Chapter 2, section 1a).

They must show that they can teach 'the objectives in the National Literacy and Numeracy Strategy frameworks competently and independently' (*QTS Standards*, TTA, 2002a, Chapter 3, section 2, sub-section 2a).

For *Key Stages 1* and *2*, teachers must have a secure understanding of 'the frameworks, methods and expectations set out in the National Numeracy and Literacy Strategies' (*QTS Standards*, TTA, 2002a, Chapter 2, section 1b). They have to show that they can teach 'English, including National Literacy Strategy, mathematics through the National Numeracy Strategy . . . competently and independently' (*QTS Standards*, TTA, 2002a, Chapter 3, section 3, sub-section 2b).

'[T]his is likely to involve trainees demonstrating sufficient knowledge and understanding of all the subject content in the pupils' National Curriculum for the core subjects, and the National Literacy and Numeracy Strategies, to teach pupils of all abilities including the most able in the age range for which they are trained to teach' (*Handbook of Guidance on QTS Standards and ITT Requirements*, TTA, 2002b, Chapter 2, section 1b, scope).

In *Key Stage 3* teachers must have a secure knowledge of 'the frameworks, methods and expectations set out in the National Strategy for Key Stage 3' (*QTS Standards*, TTA, 2002a, Chapter 2, section 1c). They 'must be able to use the cross-curricular elements, such as literacy and numeracy, set out in the National Strategy for Key Stage 3 in their teaching, as appropriate, to their specialist subject' (*QTS Standards*, TTA, 2002a, Chapter 3, section 3, sub-section 2c).

This chapter indicates the importance of literacy and numeracy with regard to general learning difficulties. It then outlines the implications of the National Literacy Strategy and the National Numeracy Strategy for pupils with SEN and explains the National Literacy Strategy's three 'waves'. The chapter then sets out the implications of the National Strategy for Key Stage 3 (in so far as it concerns literacy and numeracy) in relation to pupils with SEN. Finally, it focuses on pupils with specific difficulties in literacy.

Literacy and numeracy in general learning difficulties

The Draft *Code of Practice* Threshold document (Department for Education and Employment, 2000d) gives interesting perspectives on learning difficulties. While it could be argued that the document was never finalised and therefore has limited relevance, this view is not held by all, for example, Frederickson and Cline (2002) refer extensively to it. The Threshold document suggests that general learning difficulties may be indicated by:

- low levels of attainment across the board in all forms of assessment, including, for young children, baseline assessments;
- difficulty in acquiring skills (notably literacy and numeracy) on which much other learning in school depends;
- difficulty in dealing with abstract ideas and generalising from experience;
- a range of associated difficulties notably in speech and language (particularly for younger children) and in social and emotional development.

The National Literacy Strategy and SEN

The National Literacy Strategy (NLS) in primary schools emphasises teaching literacy skills directly to the class as a whole and to small groups within the class. It has been adapted for pupils in special schools (Berger *et al.*, 1999). The NLS *Framework of Learning Objectives* specifies the content of literacy teaching covering the National Curriculum statutory requirements for reading and writing. Four strategies to access the meaning of text are noted:

- knowledge of content;
- knowledge of grammar;
- word recognition and graphic knowledge;
- phonics (sounds and spelling).

Teaching objectives relating to the strategies are provided at the word, sentence and text level.

The methodology of the 'literacy hour', encourages direct teaching and emphasises interaction between teachers and learners. Among the teaching strategies considered suitable (Department for Education and Employment, 1998b) are: direction; demonstration; discussion; modelling (e.g. through shared reading); scaffolding (e.g. using writing frames); explanation; questioning; listening and responding; initiating and guiding exploration; and investigating ideas.

The NLS document suggests that many mainstream children with SEN will be able to achieve at the age appropriate level in the NLS, 'with help and encouragement'. Most will 'benefit significantly' from being involved in class work with their peers. Even where children with SEN need to work on different objectives, they should be taught with their own class and year group.

Various ways have been suggested and developed to encourage the inclusion of pupils with SEN in the Literacy Hour in ordinary schools. These include:

- the teacher asking questions of different complexity levels (Department for Education and Employment, 1998b);
- support from a teaching assistant (Ibid.);
- appropriate systems of communication such as manual signing (Ibid.);
- special or adapted materials (Ibid.);
- groups of pupils working on 'catch-up' programmes and reading schemes where work is focused on NLS Framework objectives (preferably linked to the main class topic themes and teacher focus) during the independent work section of the Literacy Hour (Gross et al., 1999).

However, it is recognised that some pupils with SEN may need to work outside the Literacy Hour while other pupils are working in the Literacy Hour session. This may arise when extra support provided outside the Literacy Hour times or within it is insufficient (Department for Education and Employment, 1998b, p. 115). Outside the Literacy Hour, pupils with SEN may benefit from additional approaches such as:

- the Reading Recovery programme;
- cross-age peer tutoring;
- family literacy with parents and pupils working together;
- foundation building work relating to objectives from earlier NLS levels or from a different Key Stage (although this may be accommodated to some degree within the Literacy Hour).

Concerning particular interventions, a helpful report (Brooks, 2002) considers the effectiveness of evaluated intervention schemes that have been used in the United Kingdom. These interventions aim to boost reading, spelling or writing attainment of lower achieving pupils in at least one of the years 1 to 6. Among the conclusions of the report are that it is often reasonable to expect an impact sufficient to double the standard rate of progress and that several schemes have provided evidence of such an impact in at least one study. These include, for example, Reading Recovery, Phono-Graphix™ and Paired Reading.

The National Literacy Strategy's three 'waves'

The NLS implies three 'waves' of support which may be related to the graduated response outlined in the *Special Educational Needs Code of Practice* (Department for Education and Skills, 2001a). Wave one refers to the inclusion of all pupils in an effective Literacy Hour. Pupils with SEN who are included may be identified as at the point of 'School Action' or 'School Action Plus'. Wave two concerns small group intervention such as Early Literacy Support (for Year 1), Additional Literacy Support (for Years 3 and 4), Further Literacy Support (for Year 5), Booster classes and other interventions. These aim to help pupils who do *not* have SEN related directly to learning difficulties in literacy or mathematics to catch up with peers. Where pupils in wave two interventions are on 'School Action' or 'School Action Plus' or have a statement, this may relate to SEN such as emotional and behavioural difficulties, communication and interaction difficulties or sensory or physical impairment. Wave three interventions are specifically for pupils with SEN. These pupils may have SEN relating to literacy or related to other barriers to learning and are always on 'School Action' or 'School Action Plus'.

The National Numeracy Strategy and SEN

As part of the National Numeracy Strategy (NNS), all primary schools in England are expected to teach a daily mathematics lesson, much of it concentrating on numeracy. The NNS Framework sets out the curriculum for each year of Key Stages 1 and 2 giving details of the sort of activities that teachers should organise and the amount of time that should be spent on them. A standard mathematical vocabulary is encouraged.

For pupils with SEN, several suggestions were made (Department for Education and Employment, 1999c). These included the following advice to teachers: 'plan some questions specifically for pupils . . . with SEN, and ask named children to respond' (Ibid., p. 21). Where pupil's difficulties extend to mathematics, 'use the Framework to identify suitable objectives to be incorporated into individual education plans, tracking back to earlier stages if it is appropriate to do so' (Ibid., p. 23).

Pupils with hearing impairments 'may also need to sit closer to you, or to be helped to take part in the activity through signing or support given by another adult' (Ibid., p. 21). They could be 'intro-duced to the new vocabulary they will meet in next week's oral work' (Ibid., p. 22).

For pupils with physical or sensory disabilities there was believed to be no reason for them to work on a separate pro-gramme. Adaptations may be all that is necessary, for example, 'preparation for the oral and mental part of the lesson and the pace at which it is conducted, the use of signing, Braille and sym-bols, and the provision of a range of tactile materials, techno-logical aids and adapted measuring equipment' (Ibid., p. 23).

For pupils with emotional and behavioural difficulties adapta-tions 'are usually needed during the main teaching activity, with a shorter time for independent group work if adult support is not available' (Ibid., p. 23). A pupil with severe or complex difficulties 'may need to be supported with an individualised programme in the main part of the lesson' (Ibid., p. 23).

For pupils working below level 1 of the National Curriculum, guidance has been published giving examples of what pupils with SEN should be able to do at each P level (performance description level) (Department for Education and Skills, 2001e). This supple-ments guidance from the Qualifications and Curriculum Authority on planning, teaching and assessing the curriculum for pupils with learning difficulties.

Regarding working in partnership with parents a balance may need to be struck between (1) respecting parental views on how mathematics is perceived, valued and should be taught; and (2) aiming for consistency in teaching (for example, by using the recommended consistent mathematical vocabulary) to avoid too many different approaches that might be confusing to some pupils with SEN.

Also, it has been pointed out (e.g. Frederickson and Cline, 2002) that children falling behind across the board are particularly weak in processes that are normally automatic, such as solving simple addition problems without visual prompting. This may limit the range and flexibility of strategies developed by the child (Ostad, 1997).

Finally, the way that mathematical symbols are written may pose problems for pupils who confuse left and right, those having difficulties sequencing and pupils who have visual-perceptual problems.

The National Strategy for Key Stage 3: literacy, numeracy and SEN

Among the elements of the National Strategy for Key Stage 3 are approaches to improve standards in literacy and numeracy. The support materials give a flavour of the approach.

Literacy

Literacy Across the Curriculum (Department for Education and Employment, 2001b) comprises materials that may be used for in-service education and training (INSET). The overall aim is to raise literacy standards and the materials indicate how schools can 'build literacy priorities into teaching across the curriculum'. The literacy strand of the Key Stage 3 National Strategy is organised around the *Framework for Teaching English: Years 6, 7 and 8*. The *Framework* is organised in terms of word, sentence and text level objectives and gives attention to reading, writing and speaking and listening and highlights key objectives crucial to literacy development (Ibid., p. 4). All subject teachers are expected to plan, teach and mark to the key objectives. Cross-curricular priorities are identified for Years 7, 8 and 9. For example, for Year 7 an objective is 'use appropriate reading strategies to extract particular information e.g. highlighting and scanning'. In subsequent years, schools are expected to build on the work undertaken previously.

While there is some reference to inclusive classrooms, the focus is on pupils for whom English is an additional language. Where there is a particular concentration on SEN, it concerns special schools. For example, work began in relation to implications for the KS3 National Strategy for special schools through a special school pilot and a series of dissemination conferences in 2002. This included accessing the National Curriculum for mathematics through examples of what pupils with SEN should be able to do at each 'Performance Descriptor' level.

Numeracy

A *Numeracy Across the Curriculum* pack was designed to support INSET in a similar way to the approach taken for literacy across the curriculum. It was suggested that where schools have a Key

Stage 3 management group that this group should oversee development in numeracy. As part of the approach, schools devoted a whole school training day in spring 2002 seeking to improve pupils' numeracy skills and encouraging pupils to develop and use these skills appropriately in other subjects. Schools were advised to identify cross-curricular activities for each of Years 7, 8 and 9 under three priority headings:

1   to improve accuracy, particularly in calculation, measurement and graphical work;
2   to improve interpretation and presentation of graphs, charts and diagrams;
3   to improve reasoning and problem solving.
                    (Department for Education and Employment, 2001d)

Among questions that the secondary school was encouraged to consider were:

- Are all members of the SEN department familiar with teaching approaches advocated in the *Framework* for teaching mathematics, for example the approach to calculation?
- What simplifications/modifications are made for pupils with specific learning difficulties?
- Are teaching assistants aware of supporting resources, such as number lines, hundred squares, place-value charts, vocabulary checklists?
- Have you considered pre-tutoring pupils who are experiencing difficulties so that they can participate in the lesson with their peers and with a little more confidence?
                    (Ibid., Handout 3.12, Unit 3, p. 101)

Special schools or units for pupils with moderate learning difficulties or emotional and behavioural difficulties were advised to use the training pack as any other school would. In schools for pupils with severe learning difficulties or profound and multiple learning difficulties, it was recognised that much of the planning is holistic and links across the curriculum are built in. Consequently the training pack would be of limited use. However, schools for pupils with PMLD/SLD might think about other ways of linking mathematics to other subjects (Ibid., p. 5).

Specific learning difficulties in literacy

The nature of the difficulty with literacy learning is similar whether pupils have general learning difficulties or specific learning difficulties (SpLD) (Stanovich and Stanovich, 1997). The literacy content of programmes for pupils with SpLD may have much in common with that for pupils with general learning difficulties. But pupils with general learning difficulties may require differentiated work in several areas of the curriculum while pupils with SpLD in literacy may require modifications, help and support with access to learning and the curriculum and with recording their work. Given this, they would be able to work in other subjects at the same level as other pupils of the same age (Frederickson and Cline, 2002, pp. 306–7).

A report on dyslexia (British Psychological Society, 1999) indicated various theories and approaches. One of these, the 'phonological deficit/delay hypothesis', is supported by research and is implicated in several other hypotheses. Phonological processing concerns a person's ability to process sounds in spoken language. Such a processing difficulty may cause a weakness in a cognitive component of the phonological system. This may in turn influence aspects of speaking and may make it harder to form grapheme–phoneme links making the acquisition of literacy skills more difficult (Snowling, 1998). (This underlines the importance of effective, systematic phonics teaching in the NLS.) As with any hypothesis suggesting a within child 'deficit', it is necessary to recognise the importance of teaching and other environmental influences in raising attainment in literacy. Indeed, other hypotheses such as a 'learning opportunities and social context' hypothesis concentrate on environmental factors such as unsuitable learning experiences.

'Discrepancy' definitions of dyslexia relating to intelligence testing and even the often preferred approach of defining dyslexia in terms of phonology have their limitations. A strength of the definition proposed by the British Psychological Society is that it does not assume a particular hypothesis about causation but focuses on description.

> Dyslexia is evident when accurate and fluent word reading and/or spelling develops very incompletely or with great difficulty. This focuses on literacy learning at the 'word level', and implies that the problem is severe and persistent despite

appropriate learning opportunities. It provides the basis for a staged process of assessment through teaching.

(British Psychological Society, 1999, p. 5)

Indications that a pupil is having problems with accurate and fluent word reading and/or spelling include the results of end of Key Stage tests or of standardised reading and spelling tests. Alternatively, the teacher might use the objectives of the NLS Framework as a criterion-referenced assessment.

Possible reasons for the difficulties would then be explored. Taking the two earlier hypotheses as examples, one reason might be phonological delay/deficit perhaps indicated by various tests such as the Phonological Abilities test (Mutter *et al.*, 1997) or the Phonological Assessment Battery (Frederickson *et al.*, 1997).

Another reason might relate to the 'learning opportunities and social context' hypothesis (Solity, 1996) possibly indicated by evidence of poor support from parents or ineffective school teaching.

These two hypotheses suggest different approaches and views of literacy difficulties. In the phonological hypothesis one would normally review the opportunities for learning and consider that they had been appropriate before moving on to conclude that, despite this, difficulties had persisted. In the learning opportunities/ social context view, the assumption is that the learning opportunities have not been suitable. The appropriate opportunities that would be needed to address this might include elements relevant to a phonological deficit/delay view. But the problem would be considered to arise not from a within-child deficit but because of poor teaching. Approaches could include:

- gradually progressing from phonological awareness to more difficult phonic structures;
- learning phonological regularities through reading and writing and through speaking and listening;
- supporting parents through training days or workshops;
- encouraging home reading through (providing or advising parents of) suitable texts and giving guidance on strategies.

If one were to adopt the proposed BPS working definition of dyslexia, the 'learning opportunities and social context' hypothesis would not be considered to constitute dyslexia because it would indicate that 'appropriate learning opportunities' had not been provided.

In practice, the approaches indicated by the two hypotheses could be complementary. The teacher, in consultation with the SEN Co-ordinator and others, might begin by making sure that all reasonable steps were being taken to improve support from home and to ensure effective school teaching. The teacher could at the same time give appropriate emphasis to phonological approaches. Additionally, the teacher may take account of the pupil's views of his or her difficulties and his or her attitudes to reading and writing; and encourage the pupil's involvement and motivation through such strategies as involving the pupil in setting and reviewing targets for progress.

The effect of these approaches could be monitored and continuously assessed. But it may be difficult to find the right balance between adopting broad approaches considered likely to be effective and taking focused teaching approaches whose particular impact might be more easily evaluated. Should progress not be adequate, for example, should it not be sufficient to maintain or narrow the gap in attainment between the pupil and peers, specialised approaches may be used such as multi-sensory methods and phonological awareness programmes.

Chapter 7

Information and communications technology

To meet the Professional Standards for Qualified Teacher Status, teachers must demonstrate that 'They know how to use ICT effectively, both to teach their subject and to support their wider professional role' (*QTS Standards*, TTA, 2002a, Chapter 2, section 5).

'ICT has an important role to play in most aspects of teachers' work in schools: in teaching and learning for individuals, small groups and whole classes; and in planning, assessment and evaluation, administration and management.' *QTS Standard* 2.5 sets out, 'Two aspects of ICT competence which trainees can be expected to develop and demonstrate: how to best use ICT to teach the subject(s) they are trained to teach, and their own ICT skills, which will allow them to, for example, complete pupils' records of progress, prepare resources for pupils and keep to a minimum their administrative tasks' (*Handbook of Guidance on QTS Standards and ITT Requirements*, TTA, 2002b, Chapter 2, section 5, scope).

'Evidence of knowledge could also be gathered from, for example, the ways in which trainees record pupils' progress and show how ICT has enhanced pupils' learning, their ability to access resources and information in remote data bases such as the National Grid for Learning (NGfL) and their ability to select, customise and use these materials with pupils' (*Handbook of Guidance on QTS Standards and ITT Requirements*, TTA, 2002b, Chapter 2, section 5, evidence).

To meet the requirements of the Professional Standards for Qualified Teacher Status, teachers must demonstrate that 'They select and prepare resources and plan for their safe and effective organisation, taking account of pupils' interests and their language and cultural backgrounds, with the help of support staff where appropriate' (*QTS Standards*, TTA, 2002a, Chapter 3, section 1, sub-section 3).

'Teachers need to be able to select from available resources such as books and other published materials, museum and gallery resources, visual aids, tools, specialist equipment, artefacts, software, and also show that they are able to prepare their own resources where necessary. Trainees need to be able to use the advice and support of colleagues in their selection, preparation and use of resources' (*Handbook of Guidance on QTS Standards and ITT Requirements*, TTA, 2002b, Chapter 3, section 1, sub-section 3, scope).

'In subjects such as science, technology or ICT, planning for the use of resources might require trainees to be able to liaise closely with technicians' (*Handbook of Guidance on QTS Standards and ITT Requirements*, TTA, 2002b, Chapter 3, section 1, sub-section 3, evidence).

'When judging trainees teaching, assessors may wish to consider: . . . Does the trainee consult with pupils about their views on different resources and their impact on their learning and development?' (*Handbook of Guidance on QTS Standards and ITT Requirements*, TTA, 2002b, Chapter 3, section 1, sub-section 3).

'They use ICT effectively in their teaching' (*QTS Standards*, Chapter 3, section 3, sub-section 10).

'When judging trainees' teaching, assessors might wish to consider: is the trainee able to select and use software to support the teaching of subjects? Can the trainee access interactive, on-line data base content using, for example, the National Grid for Learning (NGfL) or the Teacher Resource Exchange (TRE) and select, customise and use these materials with pupils? Can the trainee provide opportunities for pupils to use ICT to find things out and make things happen? Does the trainee use ICT terminology accurately? Can the trainee make use of ICT with individuals, groups and the whole class? Does the trainee take account of copyright, reliability, privacy and confidentiality issues when preparing materials for pupils or collecting data? Can the trainee identify opportunities to use ICT with confidence without the assistance of others?' (*Handbook of Guidance on QTS Standards and ITT Requirements*, TTA, 2002b, Chapter 3, section 3, sub-section 10, evidence).

To meet the Induction Standards, NQTs should, by the end of the induction period demonstrate that they 'use ICT effectively to support their wider professional role' (*Induction Standards* (e), TTA, 2002c).

This chapter considers the effective employment of ICT with pupils with SEN drawing on expectations of the Office for Standards in Education (OfSTED) and guidance in the *Special Educational Needs Code of Practice* (Department for Education and Skills, 2001a). It mentions some of the resources available within the National Grid for Learning. It considers a selection of facilities available with ICT rendering it unnecessary to repeatedly explain them when they are given as examples later in the chapter. It looks at the use of ICT to support areas of the curriculum, particularly literacy and numeracy, and for particular areas of SEN such as emotional, behavioural and social difficulties. The two aspects inter-relate in that using ICT, for example, in literacy overlaps with its use in specific learning difficulties concerning literacy. The chapter touches on the potential disadvantages of ICT where it might predominantly occupy pupils rather than educate them and its potential to reinforce the isolation of some pupils. Finally, it outlines some general considerations in the use of ICT.

Office for Standards in Education and ICT

OfSTED judges schools according to whether they make effective use of new technologies including ICT in the leadership and management of the school (Office for Standards in Education, 1999c, p. 104). The new technologies include:

- calculators;
- CD-ROMs;
- control and sensing technology;
- data analysis;
- digital cameras;
- electronic mail;
- interactive whiteboards;
- the Internet;
- multimedia compositions;
- the National Grid for Learning;
- projectors;
- scanners;
- subject and professional software;
- video.

For example, the SEN Co-ordinator might use new technologies to keep up to date with current professional developments (the Internet), update colleagues about particular pupils with SEN (e-mail); or compile graphs or other visual representations of the progress of pupils with SEN (data analysis and presentation). He or she might keep Individual Education Plans and annual review reports up to date using software that inter-relates the information. Other teachers may use the Internet, e-mail, CD-ROM and other new technologies in the course of their professional development.

In considering how well pupils are taught, OfSTED inspectors also consider whether teachers 'use time, support staff and other resources, especially ICT, effectively' (Ibid., p. 60).

An OfSTED report on ICT in schools which considered the impact of government initiatives in primary, secondary and special schools considered that there was particular need for improvement in the effective implementation of ICT across all subjects. Among its recommendations was that there should be further development in the role of ICT in the National Literacy Strategy, the National Numeracy Strategy and the National Strategy for Key Stage 3 (Office for Standards in Education, 2002).

Special Educational Needs Code of Practice and ICT

The *Special Educational Needs Code of Practice* (Department for Education and Skills, 2001a) recognises the importance of ICT in relation to SEN. For example, at School Action Plus in the primary phase the SENCO and class teacher together with 'curriculum, literacy and numeracy co-ordinators and external specialists' should consider 'a range of different teaching approaches and appropriate equipment and teaching materials, including the use of information technology' (Ibid., Chapter 5, section 58).

Similarly, at School Action Plus for the secondary sector, 'The SENCO, link workers or subject specialists, and the literacy and numeracy co-ordinators, together with external specialists, should consider a range of different teaching approaches and appropriate equipment and teaching material, including the use of information technology' (Ibid., Chapter 6, section 6).

When a child is undergoing statutory assessment, LEAs, in the light of the child's learning difficulties, should consider the action taken. Among the questions they should ask is whether 'the school has explored the possible benefits of, and where practicable, secured access for the child to appropriate information technology . . . so that the child is able to use that technology across the curriculum in school, and where appropriate at home' (Ibid., Chapter 7, section 49). Examples of this technology and its use are:

- word processing facilities including spell checkers;
- overlay keyboards and software;

- specialised switches;
- provision of training in the use of the technology for the child, their parents and staff.

Resources in the National Grid for Learning

The National Grid for Learning (NGfL) (http://www.ngfl.gov.uk/index.html) is a gateway to educational resources on the Internet, providing a network of links to websites offering useful information. NGfL, funded by the Department for Education and Skills, is managed by the British Educational Communications Technology Agency (BECTA). A search under 'SEN' will help users begin their information search including gaining access to the sites mentioned in the remainder of this section.

The Virtual Teacher Centre is intended for school professionals and provides news, support for professional development and the facility to search for resources across the NGfL.

The Teacher Resource Exchange is a database of resources and activities aimed at helping teachers develop and share ideas for good practice. Within the resource is a section on 'inclusion' which has some entries relating to SEN.

The Communication Aids Project is funded by the Department for Education and Skills from 2002 to 2004. It works through a number of centres with LEA and other staff and aims to support the statutory provision made by local education authorities in providing ICT equipment for pupils having communication difficulties. The project will help supply aids to pupils for their own use to improve access to learning and the curriculum and encourage communication.

Examples of ICT

Voice recognition technology

Voice recognition technology turns spoken words into text. The computer can also be controlled using spoken instructions. The pupil usually speaks into a headphone microphone. Earlier versions used discrete and rather robotic speech while more sophisticated versions respond to more fluent and natural speech. It has been found that the discrete versions are sometimes more useful for pupils with language difficulties who may find it difficult to produce the necessary fluency for continuous speech. The technology requires the pupil to devote a considerable investment of time and effort to 'teach' the computer their own voice patterns and to learn the techniques for its effective use. It is likely that as the technology becomes more user friendly, it will become an even more powerful tool than it is at present.

Switch control

Switch Access to Windows may be used to achieve access to mainstream software and is frequently used to create 'hot spots' on CD-ROMs.

Predictive word processors and talking word processors

Predictive word processors predict words that will follow others, for example, through the logical structures of syntax. Using computer-generated speech, the talking word processor enables text that is typed on to the computer screen to be read back to the pupil who has written it.

Adapted or special keyboards

Keyboards may have large keys or built-in tracker balls. Key guards may be helpful for pupils who have a tremor to find the key they require. Overlay keyboards are still used even though the alternative of touch screens is preferred for some pupils.

Literacy and numeracy and ICT

ICT software for pupils with difficulties in literacy include:

- using word processing to aid in drafting, spelling and grammar checks;
- stimulating interest and increasing the motivation of reluctant readers through the use of, for example, animation, and rewarding icons and sounds;
- reinforcing phoneme–grapheme links through combining a spoken word and its graphic equivalent.

Regarding mathematical (including numeracy) difficulties, ICT software that may help includes:

- stimulating interest and increasing the motivation of pupils through, for example, animation or rewarding icons and sounds;
- reinforcing links between numerals and object clusters;
- using finely graded tasks with built in reinforcement and correction.

Mathematics processors may be used for children who understand mathematical concepts but have difficulty using compasses or protractors. The processor assists in drawing lines and shapes and allows scale or rotation to be altered by the pupil.

Particular SEN

The *Special Educational Needs Code of Practice* (Department for Education and Skills, 2001a) considered SEN under the four headings of: (1) communication and interaction; (2) cognition and learning; (3) behaviour, emotional and social development; and (4) sensory or physical difficulties.

Pupils with difficulties in communication and interaction may be assisted by the following:

- speech input and output devices, voice recognition technology;
- word processing facilities including predictive word processors;
- painting programmes;
- software encouraging communication and self-expression;
- a graphic capability such as icons and symbols or overlay keyboards for topic vocabulary;
- switch technology;
- talking books.

Pupils with cognition and learning difficulties may be helped by the following:

- overlay keyboards, on screen word banks;
- multi-media encouraging the use of several senses to assist memory and learning;

- word processing facilities including spell checkers, direct speech input, and word prediction software.

For pupils with higher levels of cognition and learning difficulties, progressive developmentally based activities for assessment and teaching may be used. These may include experimental visual and auditory stimulation; cause and effect through pressing a switch or touching a screen to create or change shape, pattern and object animation; phased switch building, timed activation, and making choices through row scanning.

Pupils with specific learning difficulties, for example, dyslexia may be helped by the following:

- assessment software;
- word processors including predictive word processors;
- software teaching touch typing;
- software reinforcing spelling patterns.

Regarding pupils with emotional, behavioural, and social development, for pupils who may be frustrated by not being able to keep pace with others, ICT may offer the opportunity to work at the pupil's pace so long as this is sufficiently challenging. The use of computers may give the opportunity to pupils having difficulties with relationships to work individually for a time. Such work may be built into the classroom routines for all pupils and perhaps used as a reward for appropriate social behaviour. This could help avoid its over-use by pupils who find relationships difficult and would avoid isolating the pupil and inhibiting opportunities to develop social and behavioural skills.

Also useful may be word processing facilities, painting programmes and other software encouraging communication and self-expression, desktop publishing, and spreadsheets.

Where behavioural, emotional and social difficulties are associated with low attainment perhaps related to school absences, software which structures and supports learning (such as a predictive word processor) may provide the initial experiences of success that will help motivate the pupil and build confidence.

Turning to sensory and physical difficulties, among the uses of ICT for pupils with hearing impairment are the following:

- word processing facilities;
- software that allows the pupil to break down words and see their construction of combinations of sound but using visual rather than auditory patterns;
- painting programmes;
- other software which uses the visual power of the computer.

Pupils with visual impairment may be helped by the following:

- voice synthesisers linked to computers;
- speech input/output;
- screen magnification software to gain access to standard software;
- Braille input and output systems;
- overlay keyboards;
- software to help develop QWERTY keyboard skills;
- web browsers that enlarge Internet web pages and speak their content;
- scanners allowing text to be scanned onto the computer then enlarged, converted into Braille or otherwise adapted.

For pupils with physical disabilities, uses of ICT include:

- special keyboards and switch input to allow access to word processing facilities and software, adaptations to overcome problems using a mouse;
- speech recognition software;
- head pointers or head mice (e.g. optical);
- predictive word processors;
- tracker ball and joy sticks;
- overlay or on-screen 'keyboards';
- the Internet.

Virtual reality architectural simulations of a school have been used to help pupils in wheelchairs plan and practise routes through the school and gain 'experience' of them before physically attempting the routes themselves.

General considerations

Certain general points may be considered when using ICT to aid access to learning and the curriculum and to improve communication. A careful assessment of the teaching and learning needs of the pupil will fully involve the pupil and take account of their views and preferences. This will involve parents and perhaps a range of professionals such as teachers, the SENCO, a speech therapist, physiotherapist and others. The time taken for training and the cost of training must be built into planning for the long-term use of ICT. Staff working with the pupil should be confident and competent in the use of the equipment concerned. The effectiveness of the use of ICT should be monitored and evaluated in the same way that any intervention is. The whole approach should have a clear rationale against which progress is assessed.

It is important to remember that ICT is a tool. The educational aims of the lesson should take priority and ICT should be used when it facilitates these aims. This helps to avoid the possibility that ICT may come to be used as a means of occupying pupils rather than educating them or aiding access to learning and the curriculum.

When working with an ICT technician, the main focus for the teacher should be the purpose of ICT in meeting the lesson aims and the teacher will need to convey this clearly. It is also important that the teacher is clear about which stage of the lesson ICT support will be needed.

BECTA maintain regularly updated information on their Internet site which includes fact sheets concerning ICT and particular SEN such as dyslexia, hearing impairment and physical disabilities.

Chapter 8

Resources

To meet the requirements of the Professional Standards for Qualified Teacher Status, teachers must demonstrate that 'They select and prepare resources and plan for their safe and effective organisation, taking account of pupils' interests and their language and cultural backgrounds, with the help of support staff where appropriate' (*QTS Standards*, TTA, 2002a, Chapter 3, section 1, sub-section 3).

'Teachers need to be able to select from available resources such as books and other published materials, museum and gallery resources, visual aids, tools, specialist equipment, artefacts, software, and also show that they are able to prepare their own resources where necessary. Trainees need to be able to use the advice and support of colleagues in their selection, preparation and use of resources' (*Handbook of Guidance on QTS Standards and ITT Requirements*, TTA, 2002b, Chapter 3, section 1, sub-section 3, scope).

'In subjects such as science, technology or ICT, planning for the use of resources might require trainees to be able to liaise closely with technicians' (*Handbook of Guidance on QTS Standards and ITT Requirements*, TTA, 2002b, Chapter 3, section 1, sub-section 3, evidence).

'When judging trainees teaching, assessors may wish to consider: . . . Does the trainee consult with pupils about their views on different resources and their impact on their learning and development?' (*Handbook of Guidance on QTS Standards and ITT Requirements*, TTA, 2002b, Chapter 3, section 1, sub-section 3, evidence).

Teachers must demonstrate that 'They organise and manage the physical teaching space, tools, materials and texts and other resources safely and effectively with the help and support of support staff where appropriate' (*QTS Standards*, Chapter 3, section 3, sub-section 8).

This chapter considers the range of suitable resources for pupils with SEN, resources associated with the graduated response to SEN and resources associated with statutory assessment and statements (Department for Education and Skills, 2001a). It considers expectations of the Office for Standards in Education and related matters before looking at some practical aspects of the classroom environment and the choice of learning resources.

The range of resources

Among materials and resources associated with SEN (Farrell, 2002, classified index) are:

- adaptive equipment;
- aids to learning;
- Braille and Braillers;
- buildings and design;
- information and communications technology (see Chapter 7);
- journals and other publications;
- multi-sensory environments;
- play areas;
- protective appliances and clothing.

Additionally, human resources (see Chapter 12) include the teacher, teaching assistants, the SEN Co-ordinator and professionals usually

external to the school such as the educational psychologist, physiotherapist, speech and language therapist and others.

Resources in general and the graduated response to SEN

The diversity of resources is recognised in the *Special Educational
Needs Code of Practice* (Department for Education and Skills,
2001a). A critical success factor is that 'the culture, practice, management and deployment of resources in a school or setting are
designed to ensure all children's needs are met' (Ibid., Chapter 1,
section 6). Strategic planning partnerships involve a range of
formal planning opportunities relating to all pupils including those
with SEN. Some plans open the way to resources via specific grants
(Ibid., Chapter 1, section 8). Among the duties of the governing
body are that all governors should be 'up to date and knowledgeable about the school's SEN provision, including how funding,
equipment and personnel resources are deployed' (Ibid., Chapter 1,
section 22).

In early education settings, careful thought should be given to the
time that is allocated to the SENCO, 'in the light of the *Code* and
in the context of the resources available to the setting'. In relation
to Early Years Action, it is important to consider the resources
that are associated with the provision. This may not always be
one-to-one tuition but might include 'extra adult time in devising
the nature of the planned intervention and monitoring its effectiveness; the provision of different learning materials or special equipment; some individual or group support or staff development and
training to introduce more effective strategies' (Ibid., Chapter 4,
section 26). Special educational provision for children under
compulsory school age may involve the child transferring to a
specialist provision but in most instances 'there should be a decision
that the child can attend, or continue to attend, mainstream early
education provision, but with additional support or resources'
(Ibid., Chapter 4, section 51).

As part of the graduated response to SEN in the primary phase,
schools should, unless it is an exceptional case, 'make full use of
all available classroom and school resources before expecting to
call upon outside resources' (Ibid., Chapter 5, section 20). If a
school refers a child for statutory assessment, 'they should provide
the LEA with a record of their work with the child including the

resources or special arrangements they have already made avail-able' (Ibid., Chapter 5, section 24). Part of the SENCO's role is to collaborate with curriculum co-ordinators so that 'the learning for all children is given equal priority, and available resources are used to maximum effect' (Ibid., Chapter 5, section 31). Governing bodies and head teachers should give careful thought to the SEN-CO's timetable, 'in the light of the *Code* and in the context of the resources available to the school' (Ibid., Chapter 5, section 33). When the school requests a statutory assessment, the LEA will need clear documentation relating to the child's SEN, and any action taken to deal with the needs, 'including any resources or special arrangements put in place' (Ibid., Chapter 5, section 62).

The graduated response in secondary schools assumes that 'schools should make full use of available classroom and school resources before, where necessary, bringing increasing specialist expertise to bear on the difficulties that a pupil may be experi-encing' (Ibid., Chapter 6, section 22). Where schools refer pupils for statutory assessment, they should make available to the LEA, 'a record of their work with the pupil, including the resources or special arrangements already available to the pupil' (Ibid., Chapter 6, section 26, see also Chapter 6, section 71). Part of the SENCO's role is to collaborate with heads of department or faculty, the literacy and numeracy co-ordinators and pastoral col-leagues, 'to ensure that learning for all pupils is given equal prior-ity, and that available resources are used to maximum effect' (Ibid., Chapter 6, section 34).

Resources and statutory assessments and statements

Turning to requests for statutory assessment, a school or setting may conclude that 'after they have taken action to meet the learn-ing difficulties of a child, that the child's needs remain so sub-stantial that they cannot be met effectively within the resources normally available to the school or setting' (Ibid., Chapter 7, section 9). Parents may request a statutory assessment, 'if they believe that their child has needs which are either not being met through school-based intervention, or are so substantial that a mainstream school could not meet them effectively from within their own resources' (Ibid., Chapter 7, section 23). The LEA should consider the case for statutory assessment where the balance of evidence presented to and assessed by the LEA suggests that the child's learning difficulties 'have not responded to relevant and purposeful measures taken by the school or setting and external specialists' and 'may call for special educational provision which cannot reasonably be provided within the resources normally available to mainstream maintained schools and settings in the area' (Ibid., Chapter 7, section 50). LEAs consider evidence relating to whether or not it is necessary to carry out a statutory assessment. In doing so they should bear in mind, 'the particular requirements of the individual child, and whether these requirements can be met from the resources already available to mainstream schools and settings in the area in the context of school-based intervention, monitoring and review arrangements' (Ibid., Chapter 7, section 54).

A statutory assessment may confirm that the assessment and provision made by the school or setting are appropriate but that the child is not progressing or not progressing sufficiently. The LEA then has to consider what further provision may be needed and whether it can be made within the resources of the school or setting or whether a statement is necessary. The LEA may consider that the school could make certain provision from within its own resources through School Plus. This may apply (depending on specific circumstances and funding arrangements in the area) if a child needed:

- occasional/irregular advice from an external specialist;
- occasional/irregular support with personal care;
- access to a particular piece of equipment such as an electronic keyboard; or
- minor building alterations such as improving the acoustic environment.

On the other hand, the LEA may consider that the school could not reasonably be expected to make certain provision from within its own resources and may decide to issue a statement. This may apply (depending on specific circumstances and funding arrangement in the area) if a child needed:

- regular/frequent direct teaching by a specialist teacher;
- daily individual support from a learning support assistant;

- a 'significant' piece of equipment such as a closed circuit television; or
- the regular involvement of non-educational agencies.

(See Ibid., Chapter 8, section 13)

The LEA draws up a statement of SEN when it decides that, 'the special educational provision necessary to meet the child's needs cannot reasonably be provided within the resources normally available to mainstream schools and early education settings in the area' (Ibid., Chapter 8, section 2). Where extra resources are required to enable a school to make the provision specified in a statement, the LEA may do the following:

- provide the resources directly from central provision;
- devolve them to schools, 'on an ear-marked basis', or
- delegate them.

Office for Standards in Education expectations and related matters

In school inspections, and when schools are using the OfSTED guidance for school self-evaluation, a question relating to how well the school teaches its pupils is, 'Do teachers use time, support staff and other resources, especially information and communications technology, effectively?' 'The management of pupils' time, resources and support promotes good behaviour and effective learning.' Also, resources should be 'sufficient in quantity and quality, and fitted to the intended work'. Teachers are expected to manage time and resources so that pupils work productively (Office for Standards in Education, 1999, p. 60).

In considering how well the school is led and managed, inspectors judge the following:

- the extent to which the school makes best strategic use of its resources, including specific grants and additional funding, linking decisions on spending to educational priorities (Ibid., p. 103);
- the extent to which the principles of best value are applied in the use of the school's resources (Ibid., p. 105);
- the adequacy of staffing, accommodation and learning resources (Ibid., p. 106).

In practical terms, when teaching pupils with SEN, this translates into the teacher ensuring that the following are used effectively:

- time;
- support staff;
- other resources, especially ICT.

Using time effectively with regard to pupils with SEN could include such things as having a suitable pace for lessons that will maintain interest but allow for necessary consolidation and ensuring that any special equipment needed is available and in good working order.

The effective use of support staff such as a teaching assistant includes ensuring that the teachers and teaching assistant share planning where possible. At the very least, the teacher should ensure that the teaching assistant is clear about the learning objective of the lesson as a whole and the particular learning outcomes of any pupils with whom he or she is specifically working. A cycle of assessment and planned subsequent teaching should be established.

The use of ICT was considered in Chapter 7. The teacher should ensure that within the resources available in the school the classroom resources used for particular lessons are 'sufficient in quantity and quality, and fitted to the intended work'. This includes considering the lesson aims and learning outcomes carefully and ensuring that the choice of materials, use of staff and pupil organisation all facilitate achieving the necessary outcomes. For example, if the aim at some point in the lesson is to encourage discussion, is an arrangement of furniture that will accommodate small groups appropriate?

Careful planning and a close attention to lesson objectives and proposed learning outcomes will help ensure that the teacher is able to select and prepare resources. Planning for the safe and effective organisation of resources may be helped if the teacher mentally runs through the whole sequence of the lesson step by step. In doing this they may note what is needed, when it is necessary for pupils to move around the classroom, where equipment can be most safely kept and what routines are necessary for its safe use.

Taking account of pupils' interests and their language and cultural backgrounds includes being aware of the particular needs of all pupils, including those with SEN, and working closely with other staff as appropriate, including staff who support pupils for whom English is an additional language.

The classroom environment and learning resources

The physical teaching space of the classroom is important for all children, including those with SEN. The physical environment, which is a facet of the classroom as a learning environment, is to varying degrees within the control of the teacher. A primary teacher with a classroom base or secondary teacher with a subject base are better placed to improve the environment than a teacher who has to move from class to class throughout a typical week.

Basic characteristics of a good classroom include general tidiness, effective displays including displays of pupils' work, and equipment having its 'home base' known and respected by all pupils. Also important are a proper regard for safety, and furniture chosen for its practicability (for example, tables that can be put together in various ways to support individual or group work) (Farrell *et al.*, 1995, pp. 132–133).

Particular modifications to the classroom environment or special care with aspects of the environment may be necessary for some pupils with SEN. For example, pupils with sensory difficulties may need 'appropriate seating, acoustic conditions and lighting' (Department for Education and Skills, 2001a, Chapter 7, section 62). More nebulously, but very importantly, pupils with emotional, social and behavioural difficulties may require 'the provision of a safe and supportive environment' (Ibid., Chapter 7, section 60). This relates to a safe psychological environment in which a pupil can express feelings and in which behaviour can be safely managed as well as to a safe physical environment.

Selecting learning resources may appear daunting at first, not least because of the plethora available from commercial and other sources. However, a few guiding principles can narrow down the range of resources that may be suitable for pupils with SEN.

The main focus is the learning objectives associated with medium and short-term planning. Resources are only useful if they facilitate the learning objectives set for pupils. Commercial resources do not always start from this point of view because an important if obvious objective is to sell the resource. They may therefore seek to set up a need in the teacher or school to buy the resource that is not always central to important learning objectives. Such selling strategies may emphasise the up-to-date nature of the resource or may play on certain anxieties the new teacher may have, perhaps relating to controlling the difficult behaviour of some pupils.

Materials previously catalogued by the publisher as suitable for younger pupils may suddenly appear as suitable for older pupils with SEN. This begs many questions about interest level, motivation and age appropriateness of the resources.

Similarly, when reviewing museum and gallery resources, the starting point is not considering what is available, but what learning objectives are to be fulfilled by the materials. Advice from the museum or gallery education officer can then be more precise and helpful because it will be more focused on the teacher's requirements related to the pupils' learning.

Consulting with pupils about how they view different resources and how these help them to learn does not imply the teacher asking the pupil what resources to use. Rather, it suggests that, having determined the learning outcomes of a lesson and made a professional choice of resources, the teacher will consult with the pupil about whether the resources are helpful, stimulating, interesting, and so on.

This may reveal pupil preferences for resources that the teacher may not have thought of but that might nevertheless help achieve the learning objectives of the lesson just as well or better than the resources that the teacher did deploy.

At all times the trainee teacher and the newly qualified teacher should be ready to discuss with colleagues their choice of resources and seek advice on alternatives that might support similar learning objectives.

Chapter 9

Emotional, behavioural and social difficulties

To meet the Professional Standards for Qualified Teacher Status, teachers must demonstrate that 'They identify and support more able pupils, those working below age related expectations, those who are failing to achieve their potential in learning, and those who experience behavioural, emotional and social difficulties' (*QTS Standards*, TTA, 2002a, Chapter 3, section 2, sub-section 4).

'[T]rainees might use classroom observation to assess attention and concentration, to note how the pupil works with others, and to identify simple explanatory patterns behind behaviour and learning difficulties such as extreme shyness, withdrawn behaviour in certain contexts, or poor concentration' (*Handbook of Guidance on QTS Standards and ITT Requirements*, TTA, 2002b, Chapter 3, section 2, sub-section 4, evidence).

Teachers must demonstrate that 'They know a range of strategies to promote good behaviour' (*QTS Standards*, TTA, 2002a, Chapter 2, section 7).

'Trainees could also demonstrate their knowledge of effective behaviour management by the approaches they use in the classroom, for example: teaching assertively, maintaining a brisk pace to their lessons, setting and maintaining high expectations, using their voice effectively, using praise and encouragement, asking carefully formulated questions, and intervening in a timely way to maintain or refocus pupils on task. In addition, trainees' work with classroom assistants and other adults could indicate they know how to deploy such support to establish a purposeful learning environment' (*Handbook of Guidance on QTS Standards and ITT Requirements*, TTA, 2002b, Chapter 2, section 7, evidence).

Teachers must demonstrate that 'They set high expectations for pupils' behaviour and establish a clear framework for classroom discipline to anticipate and manage pupils' behaviour constructively and promote self-control and independence' (*QTS Standards*, TTA, 2002a, Chapter 3, section 3, sub-section 9).

'When judging trainees' teaching, assessors may wish to consider, for example: can the trainee identify pupils responding appropriately to instructions ("catching them being good") and reinforce this behaviour through positive private or public feedback? Can the trainee identify, with the pupils, clear classroom rules and routines and apply them fairly and consistently? When dealing with incidents, can the trainee provide pupils with opportunities to reflect upon the consequences of specific behaviours? In pre-empting misbehaviour, does the trainee ensure, for example, that tasks and activities are relevant, differentiated, clearly set and understood by all pupils, and that time and resources are managed effectively? Does the trainee draw upon a range of strategies for grouping pupils according to the nature of the task, focusing and refocusing them on task and organising physical and human resources to maximise learning opportunities?' (*Handbook of Guidance on QTS Standards and ITT Requirements*, TTA, 2002b, Chapter 3, section 3, sub-section 9, evidence).

To meet *Induction Standards* (k), NQTs should, by the end of the induction period demonstrate that they 'independently differentiate their teaching to meet the needs of pupils including, where appropriate, . . . those experiencing emotional, behavioural and social difficulties' (*Induction Standard* (k), TTA, 2002c).

To meet *Induction Standards* (n), NQTs should, by the end of the induction period, demonstrate that they 'secure a good standards of pupil behaviour in the classroom and act to pre-empt and deal with inappropriate behaviour in the context of the behaviour policy of the school' (*Induction Standards* (k), TTA, 2002c).

This chapter considers a general approach to promoting appropriate behaviour. It examines the identification and support of pupils with emotional, social and behavioural difficulties (ESBD). It then looks at different perspectives on EBSD, considering behavioural, cognitive, systems and psychodynamic perspectives. The chapter considers in the light of these perspectives the definitions within the *Special Educational Needs Code of Practice* (Department for Education and Skills, 2001a).

General approaches to managing behaviour

The quotations provided in the box indicate some of the approaches suited to creating and maintaining good classroom behaviour. These include making observations of behaviour and seeking explanations for it as well as acting to promote good behaviour. Interventions include the following:

- reinforcing positive pupil behaviour;
- agreeing with pupils the classroom rules and applying them impartially;
- giving pupils the opportunity to reflect on the consequences of their particular behaviour;

- ensuring activities are relevant, differentiated, clearly set and understood by all pupils;
- making sure that time and resources are managed effectively;
- using various strategies for grouping pupils, depending on the task;
- keeping pupils focused on the task in hand;
- organising resources to optimise learning.

The teacher should read and ensure that he or she clearly understands the school behaviour policy and should strive to use the rewards and sanctions agreed by the school. Rewards normally used in the school may include pupils being mentioned in achievement and effort assemblies, a letter to parents or reporting good work or behaviour in home-school books.

Although general approaches to managing behaviour for a context in which provision for pupils with ESBD may be made, it should be recognised that pupils with ESBD by definition tend not to respond sufficiently to the usual approaches employed to encourage good behaviour in the school. The following sections therefore look at a range of approaches that have been used with pupils with ESBD.

Identification, support and intervention from a behavioural perspective

Interventions for pupils with ESBD using a behavioural approach do not assume, as is sometimes supposed, that the difficulty is exclusively within the child. Rather, it is considered that the environment has played an important part in shaping the child's behaviour. Inappropriate behaviour such as bullying or verbal abuse has been learned and reinforced by events which the child exhibiting the aggressive behaviour finds desirable (attention from parents and the teacher and 'respect' from some children). If these reinforcing events can be systematically and consistently modified, the aggressive behaviour will tend to diminish.

Identifying inappropriate behaviour is not difficult for the teacher, indeed, it is often all too apparent. However, a behavioural approach requires precision in observing and describing the behaviour. Observations may be made by the teacher, a learning support assistant, a parent, an educational psychologist or others. Whoever observes needs to be very clear what it is that they are observing. The behaviour has to be specified clearly (e.g. the child gets out of his seat without permission for a reason unconnected with the aims of the lesson). The duration and frequency of the behaviour and the setting in which it occurs are recorded to act as a baseline from which to judge the effects of subsequent interventions. The events that preceded and succeeded the inappropriate behaviour may be recorded as evidence of what might precipitate or reinforce the behaviour.

A few examples of approaches to modify behaviour (reinforcement, generalisation and shaping) are given below (see Farrell, 2002, for further techniques). The methods involve seeking to eliminate unacceptable behaviour but also encouraging appropriate behaviour such as suitable social skills.

Reinforcement relates to the consequences of a behaviour which will affect its frequency. Positive reinforcement such as a reward tends to increase the frequency of the behaviour with which it is associated. In negative reinforcement an unpleasant stimulus is removed when a desired behaviour occurs so that the learner modifies behaviour to avoid the unpleasant stimulus. Punishment involves linking an unpleasant stimulus with an unacceptable behaviour. In extinction the reinforcers of unacceptable behaviour are eliminated. For example, screaming may be reinforced by adult attention. Denying this at the same time as ensuring the learner's safety would tend to reduce the incidence of screaming. Reinforcers may be primary such as food or secondary, for example, praise. Successful reinforcers are immediate, consistent, and exclusively associated with the desired behaviour. A comprehensive approach may involve reinforcing desired behaviour and avoiding reinforcing undesirable behaviour.

Generalisation occurs when behaviour learnt in one situation happens spontaneously in another situation. A pupil taught the appropriate social behaviour of queuing in a self-service restaurant will eventually know how to queue in other similar venues.

Shaping involves developing existing behaviour. If the behaviour required is for a pupil to greet others politely, reinforcement would be given for slight, early efforts to do so. Gradually closer approximation of the target behaviour would next be required until the target behaviour was achieved.

A behavioural approach does not assume that all pupils, for example, pupils from different ethnic backgrounds, respond in the same way to the same consequences. Praise may be a positive reinforcement for some but not others. A particular punishment may decrease an undesirable behaviour in one pupil but not in another. The different interventions are defined according to their effects. Written behavioural contracts are sometimes used in which the pupil, parents, teachers and others agree on required changes in behaviour and how these changes will be supported and encouraged. If elements of a behavioural approach are to be used, it is important that:

- the undesirable behaviour is specified;
- the behaviour that it is intended should replace the unacceptable behaviour is specified;
- the consequences of not demonstrating the unpredictable behaviour are clear;
- the consequences are immediate and consistent.

Identification, support and intervention from a cognitive perspective

Cognitive approaches concern how individuals perceive and interpret events and how this involves thinking, planning and problem solving in everyday situations, the child's attribution of the causes of events (e.g. 'whose fault?'), self-perception; self-esteem and attitudes. Such negative perceptions may have their origins in past events where real hostility was experienced. They may be supported by peers in a sub-culture having different values to those of the school. Negative interpretations of events that lead to the pupil behaving anti-socially may lead to rejection by other pupils and to the teacher having a negative view of the pupil. This in turn may feed the negative self-perceptions of the pupil concerned setting up a vicious circle.

Assessment relating to cognition includes questionnaires and other methods assessing such features as self-perception and attribution. An example is the 'self-perception profile for children' (Harter, 1985). Difficulties with such assessments include that the pupil's responses may be influenced by him wanting to present himself in a positive light or that he may not sufficiently understand the language used.

Intervention includes anxiety management where children are trained to recognise early signs of anxiety (such as rapid heartbeat) and intervene through using an internal monologue, self-talk. For example, they may begin to recognise that situations which might at first be perceived as threatening and indicating the hostility or dislike of others may be perceived, perhaps more accurately, in a more positive way. More generally, intervention may involve approaches which do the following:

- question the child's misperceptions or incorrect beliefs;
- seek to reassign negative attributions;
- help develop more flexible ways of perceiving themselves and events;
- seek to replace negative defeatist self-talk with a positive equivalent.

A study by Reid and Borkowski (1987) concerned the behaviour of pupils considered 'hyperactive' and who might be considered today to exhibit attention deficit hyperactivity disorder. Of the three groups concerned:

- group 1 received training in using memory strategies;
- group 2 received training in using memory strategies and training in self-control strategies;
- group 3 received training in using memory strategies, training in self-control strategies and attribution training.

After six sessions, group 3 who received the attribution training demonstrated lower levels of impulsivity which continued to be lower ten months later.

Because cognition is influenced by others, cognitive approaches may be supplemented by work with peers and teachers so that if interventions do lead to, for example, more appropriate social behaviour, then this is recognised by others.

Identification, support and intervention from a systems perspective

Systems approaches draw on notions of the holistic and the interactive and of mutual causality. ESBD is seen as relating to mismatches in the aims and expectations of participants (e.g. pupil, parents, teachers).

Assessments involve a broad examination of a problematic situation such as conflicts between a pupil and a teacher. One then considers the attitudes, views, emotions and behaviours of the pupil, the teacher and others about the situation so that these are clearly identified. Sociometric assessment might be used to gather and collate information from others in the pupil's class(es) (see Frederickson and Cline, 2002, pp. 437–439, for examples). To try to capture some of the interaction that takes place between different pupils and different aspects of their environment (school, class groups, home, community), so-called circular questioning may be used. This involves a small group, perhaps the pupil, the teachers, parents and others, in which each are asked to focus on the thoughts, emotions and behaviour of the others and how they might interact (e.g. Dowling and Osborne, 1994).

Having conducted a broad assessment of the situation and identified different perspectives, the intervention then involves devising a plan to improve the situation to which all participants can agree and that may involve actions on the part of those concerned. This may include setting up a temporary new system, perhaps supported by a written contract. Circle time may also contribute (Kelly, 1999) by allowing groups of pupils and teachers to discuss problems and seek a multi-level solution to promoting appropriate behaviour.

A 'framework for intervention' (Daniels and Williams, 2000) adopts a systematic interactional approach to addressing behaviour problems at different levels, initially concentrating on behaviour environment plans aimed at classroom and school factors and later, as necessary, additionally developing individual behaviour plans.

Identification, support and intervention from a psychodynamic perspective

Psychodynamic perspectives are developmental and regard ESBD as a manifestation of unconscious conflicts often relating back to very early childhood experiences. Inappropriate behaviours are sometimes regarded as defence mechanisms allowing the child to avoid recognising and facing internal conflicts. The way to address the difficult behaviour or emotional difficulty is to identify and resolve the underlying conflicts. Other adults and other children in the child's world similarly act in ways affected by unconscious conflicts.

Assessment methods include projective techniques aiming to elicit responses that might indicate internal conflicts using special stimuli such as ambiguous shapes, drawings or sentences to complete. From such techniques a hypothesis that might be further explored may emerge.

For very severe ESBD one intervention is individual psychotherapy, in which, in a series of sessions often continuing for many months or sometimes years, the child is enabled to resolve inner conflicts. A few residential special schools sometimes known as therapeutic communities use psychotherapeutic interventions in day-to-day group living. An example in England is the Mulberry Bush School in Oxfordshire whose approach originally developed from the work of Donald Winnicott, a psychoanalyst and paediatrician, who placed particular importance on early mother–child bonding. Several professions use insights relating to psychodynamic approaches among which are music, art and play therapists. Teachers and others may develop through training an understanding of behaviours that may indicate internal conflicts and perhaps offer opportunities for these to be expressed and explored.

The *Special Educational Needs Code of Practice* view of ESBD

Having considered behavioural, cognitive, systems and psychodynamic perspectives, it will now be helpful to look at the perspective of ESBD in the *Special Educational Needs Code of Practice* (Department for Education and Skills, 2001a). The *Code* indicates possible triggers for Early Years Action including: 'the practitioner's or parent's concern about a child who, despite receiving appropriate educational experiences . . . presents persistent emotional and/or behavioural difficulties, which are not ameliorated by the behaviour management techniques usually employed in the setting' (*Code*, Chapter 4, section 21).

For School Action Plus, the triggers for seeking outside help could be that 'despite receiving an individualised programme and/ or concentrated support, the child . . . has emotional or behavioural difficulties which substantially or regularly interfere with the child's own learning or that of the group, despite having an individualised behaviour management programme' (Ibid., Chapter 4, section 31).

In the primary phase, School Action triggers could be 'the teacher's or others' concern, underpinned by evidence, about a child who despite receiving differentiated learning opportunities: . . .

presents persistent emotional or behaviour difficulties which are not ameliorated by the behaviour management techniques usually employed in the school' (Ibid., Chapter 5, section 44).

School Action Plus triggers could be that:

despite receiving an individualised programme and/or concentrated support under School Action, the child: . . . has emotional or behavioural difficulties which substantially and regularly interfere with the child's own learning or that of the class group, despite having an individualised behaviour management programme.

(Ibid., Chapter 5, section 56)

In the secondary sector, School Action triggers (Ibid., Chapter 6, section 51) and School Action Plus triggers (Ibid., Chapter 6, section 64) are practically identical to those in the primary phase.

Turning to statutory assessment of SEN, when an LEA is deciding whether to carry out such an assessment, it should:

seek evidence of any identifiable factors that could impact on learning outcomes including: . . . evidence of significant emotional or behavioural difficulties, as indicated by clear recorded examples of withdrawn or disruptive behaviour; a marked and persistent inability to concentrate; signs that the child experiences considerable frustration or distress in relation to their learning difficulties; difficulties in establishing and maintaining balanced relationships with their fellow pupils or with adults; and any other evidence of a significant delay in the development of life and social skills.

(Ibid., Chapter 7, section 43)

In the light of evidence about the child's learning difficulty, the LEA should consider the action taken and particularly should ask whether 'the school has implemented its policy on pastoral care and guidance and sought external advice to meet any social, emotional or behavioural difficulties' (Ibid., Chapter 7, section 49).

In referring to behavioural, emotional and social development, in relation to statutory assessment, the *Code* mentions children and young people: 'who demonstrate features of emotional and behavioural difficulties; who are withdrawn or isolated, disruptive and disturbing, hyperactive and lack concentration; those with immature skills; and those presenting challenging behaviours arising from other complex needs'.

The *Code* states that such pupils may require help or counselling for some, or all, of the following:

- flexible teaching arrangements;
- help with development of social competence and emotional maturity;
- help in adjusting to school expectations and routines;
- help in acquiring the skills of positive interaction with peers and adults;
- specialised behavioural and cognitive approaches;
- re-channelling and re-focusing to diminish repetitive and self-injurious behaviours;
- provision of class and school systems which control or censure negative or difficult behaviours and encourage positive behaviour;
- provision of a safe and supportive environment.

(Ibid., Chapter 7, section 60)

The LEA has to consider whether these interventions can be provided through School Action Plus or whether it needs to undertake a statutory assessment.

The *Code* also notes that 'Many children with mental health problems, but by no means all, may also be recognised as children with emotional and behavioural difficulties' (Ibid., Chapter 10, section 27).

Developing one's teaching

To meet the Professional Standards for Qualified Teacher Status, teachers must demonstrate that 'They understand how pupils' learning can be affected by their physical, intellectual, linguistic, social, cultural and emotional development' (*QTS Standards*, TTA, 2002a, Chapter 2, section 4).

Regarding the 'complex factors which influence individual pupils' ability to learn', trainees should have 'sufficient understanding of some of these factors to take account of and respond to individual pupil needs, to plan lessons sensitively, and to teach in an inclusive way that recognises pupils have different motivations to learn and that pupils have different needs at different times' (*Handbook of Guidance on QTS Standards and ITT Requirements*, TTA, 2002b, Chapter 2, section 4, scope).

Trainees' knowledge in relation to *QTS Standard* 2.4 will be indicated in their lesson planning and teaching and the 'strategies they use for differentiation, the approaches they take to organising groups, their selection of resources and their setting of pupil targets will be useful areas of focus' (*Handbook of Guidance on QTS Standards and ITT Requirements*, TTA, 2002b, Chapter 2, section 4, evidence).

Teachers must demonstrate that 'They set challenging teaching and learning objectives which are relevant to all pupils in their classes. They base these on their knowledge of:

- the pupils
- evidence of their past and current achievement' (*QTS Standards*, TTA, 2002a, Chaapter 3, section 1, subsection 1).

In relation to *QTS Standard* 3.1.1, 'Direct observation of teaching and pupils' responses will provide evidence of how well the objectives are matched to the pupils', and when judging trainees' teaching, assessors will want to consider, 'Do the objectives take account of a range of needs and attainment?' (*Handbook of Guidance on QTS Standards and ITT Requirements*, TTA, 2002b, Chapter 3, section 1, subsection 1).

Teachers must demonstrate that 'They take account of and support pupils' varying needs so that girls and boys, from all ethnic groups can make good progress' (*QTS Standards*, TTA, 2002a, Chapter 3, section 1, sub-section 2).

'They identify and support more able pupils, those working below age related expectations, those who are failing to achieve their potential in learning, and those who experience behavioural, emotional and social difficulties' (*QTS Standards*, TTA, 2002a, Chapter 3, section 2, sub-section 4).

'When judging trainees' teaching, assessors might consider, for example; does the trainee seek information from colleagues such as the SEN Co-ordinator, and/or pupils' parents or carers to gain information, where necessary, about pupils' strengths and difficulties? Can the trainee identify the contexts in which the pupil learn effectively, and use these to help planning and teaching, drawing on guidance from experienced staff where appropriate? Does the trainee demonstrate in their teaching that they can, with support, employ appropriate teaching strategies and devise tasks and activities to support the learning both of the more able and those working below age related expectations?' (*Handbook of Guidance on QTS Standards and ITT Requirements*, TTA, 2002b, Chapter 3, section 2, sub-section 4).

Teachers must demonstrate that they 'differentiate their teaching to meet the needs of pupils, including the more able and those with special educational needs. They may have guidance from an experienced teacher where appropriate' (*QTS Standards*, TTA, 2002a, Chapter 3, section 3, sub-section 4).

'If trainees work in a school that has a unit for pupils with impaired vision or hearing, they might present evidence on how they differentiate their teaching to meet the needs of one or more such pupils. Records of pupils' progress provide trainees with the opportunity to explain how their teaching takes account of the Individual Education Plans of pupils with special educational needs' (*Handbook of Guidance on QTS Standards and ITT Requirements*, TTA, 2002b, Chapter 3, section 3, sub-section 4, evidence).

Teachers must demonstrate that 'They are able to improve their own teaching, by evaluating it, learning from the effective practice of others and from evidence' (*QTS Standards*, TTA, 2002a, Chapter 1, section 7).

To meet *Induction Standards* (e), NQTs should, by the end of the induction period, 'plan effectively, where applicable, to meet the needs of pupils with special educational needs, with or without statements, and in consultation with the SENCO contribute to the preparation, implementation, monitoring and review of Individual Education Plans or their equivalent' (*Induction Standards* (e), TTA, 2002c).

To meet *Induction Standards* (k), NQTs should, by the end of their induction period, 'independently differentiate their teaching to meet the needs of pupils, including where appropriate, . . . those with special educational needs . . . [including] those experiencing behavioural, emotional and social difficulties' (*Induction Standards* (k), TTA, 2002c).

This chapter examines the role of the teacher as a practitioner researcher. In particular, it considers how teaching approaches are refined; how one might evaluate one's own teaching, how effective practice of others may be identified, and ways in which one might learn from that effective practice. The chapter then looks at pupil differences relating to gender, ethnicity and using English as an additional language in relation to SEN.

The role of the teacher as 'practitioner researcher'

Implicit in developing one's teaching by recording what worked and what did not and through the observation of others and other means, is a perspective of the teacher as a practitioner researcher. The research aspect is a continuing reflection of one's own performance and the learning of pupils which is used to inform one's teaching which is as much an attitude of mind as a technique.

The teacher can first take an interest in research carried out by other practitioners, perhaps consulting journals that carry research reports such as the *British Journal of Special Educational Needs*. Furthermore, the teacher may consider the importance of action research (Farrell *et al.*, 1995, pp. 18–19) which at its best powerfully combines the involvement of the practitioner with the objective standards of the researcher. Related to this is the vision of the teacher characterised as a reflective practitioner (Schön, 1987). To illustrate some of these points, the chapter examines some refined teaching approaches, evaluating one's own teaching and learning from the good practice of others.

Refining teaching approaches

Refining teaching approaches involves teaching pupils with various characteristics each according to his or her characteristics in a group setting, implying an understanding of the individual differences between children and their entitlement and access to the National Curriculum. Individual differences include prior attainment and aptitudes, as well as the pupils' learning preferences. The teacher encourages pupils' progress through the curriculum adopting appropriate teaching, curriculum and assessment approaches. For pupils with SEN this implies the inclusion of the pupil with others in the classroom but does not preclude the grouping of pupils in the classroom according to prior attainment. Developing suitable strategies involves planning curriculum objectives, teaching and assessment approaches, learning activities and resources.

Approaches to teaching include paying particular attention to outcome, delivery/task, pace/extension, level of work, recording, resources, organisation and support.

Focusing on outcome involves pupils being given the same task and content but the teacher assessing the outcome according to each pupil's level. While this may be thought to occur automatically, in order for this not to become a 'strategy' by default, planning is important. The expected outcome should be clear from the beginning and it should be sufficiently challenging while still allowing the pupil opportunities to succeed.

In concentrating on delivery or task, the learning outcomes are the same but the delivery different. In reading, one child may be working with a predominantly phonic approach while another may be using a mainly look and say approach.

Approaches taking particular note of pace or extension involve pupils being engaged in similar activities but allowing for individuals working at different speeds. Pupils who work faster need supplementary and extension work. The teacher should make it clear at the beginning of a session the expectation that specified pupils will finish the extension work in the same session. Otherwise extension tasks become optional extras and pace may not vary.

Paying particular heed to a pupil's level of work usually occurs within a set scheme, such as mathematics or reading. Individual children may be at different levels on the same scheme according to the level of previous learning.

Teaching approaches concentrating on recording are sensitive to the way in which a pupil records his or her response and allows for variations such as written responses, verbal responses or pictorial representation.

In focusing on resources, the content of the lesson is the same for all pupils but resources allow particular pupils access to learning (or they aid learning). A pencil grip may be used for a pupil with coordination difficulties. Materials such as unifix blocks may be used to aid calculations in mathematics. Visual aids such as photographs or objects may be used to help understanding.

Teaching approaches stressing organisation may involve a teacher grouping children within a classroom according to criteria such as prior attainment in the particular lesson or task, helping the allocation of resources to support learning. Pupils requiring practical aids such as a 'number line' for a mathematics task might be grouped together, enabling the necessary materials to be shared.

Pupils may receive planned support from the teacher or another adult. This can be linked to varying the organisation so that the teacher can support groups finding a particular task or area of knowledge acquisition particularly difficult. If support is to be planned for predominantly one group or several in a lesson, then if there is one teacher for the class, other groups need comparatively self-sustaining tasks. The activities and the learning for these groups should be challenging, but the work should be structured and supported by resources so as to need less teacher support.

Evaluating one's own teaching

As a trainee or a newly qualified teacher, a benefit is that one's teaching is observed and evaluated by experienced professionals and much of course can be learned from this. However, such observations are necessarily samples of teaching. If one has a way of evaluating one's teaching continually in a constructive way, there is scope for greater progress and development in teaching skills.

Lesson plans will detail what has worked and what has not and these will form a cumulative record of strategies that are successful and ones which either do not work or which require further practice and skill.

One useful model to help review teaching is that used by the Office for Standards in Education inspectors and by schools for self-evaluation (Office for Standards in Education, 1999c, 1999d). In relation to teaching pupils with SEN, it will be helpful to read through the evidence that inspectors consider when judging teaching generally and consider what might relate in particular to helping ensure the inclusion of pupils with SEN.

Learning from the effective practice of others

Another way of improving one's own teaching is to observe the teaching of others who are effective. This requires careful planning and following up if it is to be useful. One approach is to review one's own teaching strengths and weakness and draft a brief proforma identifying these. In observations the new teacher would then note how the observed teacher manages the aspects of teaching that the new teacher may be finding difficult. It will be particularly useful to observe experienced teachers in the school where the new teacher is working. They would normally be approached by the head teacher or the school-based mentor. Such observations may be informed by the new teacher's views of the areas of their own practice that they wish to improve.

In discussion with the teacher after the observed lesson, the new teacher might explore aspects of the lesson that worked well and discuss how they might be adapted in one's own lessons. For example, if class grouping is an area of weakness for the new teacher, they might discuss with the observed teacher how groupings were decided and how points of potential disruption were managed so that time was not lost as pupils physically moved from class work to group work. Careful consideration of one's own strategies can emerge from this. A key point is that skills do not automatically transfer by observing other teachers. What is required is structured observation with a purpose, followed by careful reflection on how the successful approaches might be adapted and made one's own, followed by self-critical attempts to emulate and refine the good practice.

Other observation may be arranged in other schools, including special schools where a similar structured approach could be adopted.

Pupil differences

Taking account of and supporting pupils' varying needs so that girls and boys from all ethnic groups 'can make good progress' (*QTS Standards*, Teacher Training Agency, 2002a, Chapter 3, section 1, sub-section 2) relates to SEN in various ways. Issues may arise that may be related to broad factors. These may involve concerns about progress and achievement or there may be a concern that certain pupils are over- or under-represented in terms of SEN. Factors include:

- gender;
- ethnic minority pupils;
- children for whom English is an additional language;
- social background;
- children who are looked after by the local authority;
- children who are on the child protection register.

Let us consider the first three of these factors in relation to SEN: gender, ethnicity and pupils for whom English is an additional language.

Gender and SEN

Some gender issues concern identification. In special schools for pupils with EBD, boys greatly outnumber girls (Riddell, 1996). Given the difficulty of defining EBSD (see Chapter 9), and its non-normative nature, it may be assumed that social factors may be a reason for such a discrepancy. Is one to interpret such data by considering the girls are 'under-represented' in terms of being identified as having ESBD? Or does one consider whether boys are 'over-represented'? Even to use terms such as 'under-represented' and 'over-represented' assumes that the gender balance should be about equal, an assumption that would need to be justified. For example, many more boys than girls are identified as possibly having dyslexia (Riddell *et al.*, 1994) and there is debate about the degree to which this might reflect social, biological or other factors.

Care needs to be taken that particular assessments do not unfairly favour one gender over another as this may influence views of whether the pupil has SEN or the extent to which they are making progress.

Provision appears sometimes to affect pupils according to gender. In London primary schools, one piece of research (Mortimore *et al.*, 1988) indicated that most schools had a broadly equal effect on the reading progress of both boys and girls but that in 30 per cent of schools there were gender differences in reading progress.

Ethnicity and SEN

Attempting to take account of cultural and ethnic differences in schools is not straightforward. Cultural and ethnic differences may be seen as something on which to capitalise rather than to stigmatise. But in trying to be sensitive to diversity, pupils (and others) who are identified as members of the cultural or ethnic group may be incorrectly assumed to be homogenous and to share the same traits as others of the same group (Keogh *et al.*, 1997).

A report on research considering the incidence of SEN in ordinary schools found that more children from ethnic minority backgrounds were considered to have SEN than white children. There were 50 per cent more Asian children than white children and 50 per cent more Caribbean children than white children with SEN. When behaviour difficulties were considered, there were three times as many Caribbean pupils as white pupils and half as many Asian pupils as white pupils (Croll and Moses, 1985).

If one is to speak of over-representation or under-representation in this study, the assumption might be that pupils of different ethnic backgrounds would be equally represented in SEN relating to behaviour. In the research by Croll and Moses, one may interpret the figures for Caribbean pupils as an over-representation. But then one would have to be equally concerned about the 'over-representation' of white pupils in comparison with Asian pupils. Alternatively one could take the figures for white pupils as the norm (which would need justifying) and then one might take the view that there was an 'under-representation' of Asian pupils in terms of behavioural difficulties.

More recently, a study considered SEN provision in thirty-five primary and secondary schools in two English LEAs. Black children seemed more likely to be perceived as having 'general learning difficulties' rather than 'reading difficulties' in comparison with white pupils (Daniels *et al.*, 1999).

Pupils with SEN for whom English is an additional language

In early education settings, the *Special Educational Needs Code of Practice* (Department for Education and Skills, 2001a) recommends being careful that children who are learning English as an additional language are not assumed to have SEN:

> Children making slower progress may include those who are learning English as an additional language or who have particular learning difficulties. It should not be assumed that children who are making slower progress must, therefore, have special educational needs. But such children will need carefully differentiated learning opportunities to help them progress and regular and frequent careful monitoring of their progress.
>
> (Ibid., Chapter 4, section 8)

The importance of communication with the parents of young children is recognised:

> Children with a learning difficulty or developmental delay and whose parents do not have English as a first language, do not have fluent English, or are disabled are likely to be particularly disadvantaged if any special educational needs are not identified at the earliest possible stage. Parents may be unable to voice their own concerns because of a lack of means of communication with the early education provider. Where such difficulties occur, LEAs should ensure that parents and relevant professionals are provided with access to signers or interpreters and translated information material, so that early concerns may be shared about the child's behaviour, health and development. Bilingual support staff, teachers of English as an additional language and teachers of the deaf may be able to help.
>
> (Ibid., Chapter 4, section 25)

Similarly, in the primary phase, the *Code* advises that the identification of the SEN of children whose first language is not English requires care:

> It is necessary to consider the child within the context of their home, culture and community. Where there is uncertainty about an individual child, schools should make full use of any local sources of advice relevant to the ethnic group concerned, drawing on community liaison arrangements wherever they exist.
>
> Lack of competence in English must not be equated with learning difficulties as understood in this Code. At the same time, when children who have English as an additional language make slow progress, it should not be assumed that their language status is the only reason; they may have learning difficulties. Schools should look carefully at all aspects of a child's performance in different subjects to establish whether the problems they have in the classroom are due to limitations in their command of language that is used there or arise from special educational needs. At an early stage a full assessment should be made of the exposure they have had in the past to each of the languages they speak, the use they make of them currently and their proficiency in them. The information about their language skills obtained in this way will form the basis of all further work with them both in assisting their learning and in planning any additional language support that is needed.
>
> (Ibid., Chapter 5, sections 15–16)

The advice for pupils in the secondary sector (Ibid., Chapter 6, sections 14–16) is almost identical to that of the primary phase.

Regarding statutory assessment, pupils having difficulties with communication and interaction may require (among other help): 'support to compensate for the impact of a communication difficulty on learning in English as an additional language' (Ibid., Chapter 7, section 56).

When making a statement of SEN:

> LEAs should remember the needs of parents and children whose first language is not English. Where children have

different linguistic and cultural backgrounds, LEAs should seek advice from bilingual support staff, teachers of English as an additional language, interpreters and translators and other local sources of help as appropriate, to ensure that such parents and children are involved in all aspects of the process.

(Ibid., Chapter 8, section 56)

Although there are examples of the language assessment of pupils with SEN for whom English is an additional language (e.g. Hall, 1995), there appears to be no systematic research-based approach that takes account of the diverse languages used in UK schools (Frederickson and Cline, 2002, p. 287).

A study in Scotland indicated that bilingual children and multi-lingual children are 'under-represented' in provision for dyslexia (e.g. Deponio *et al.*, 1999). This may relate in part to occasions when an intelligence-achievement model of dyslexia has been used because the validity and reliability of IQ tests have been questioned in relation to bilingual children whose English language skills are still developing.

Children from linguistic minority backgrounds tend to be referred to speech and language therapists when they are older more on average than other children experiencing the same difficulties (Winter, 1999, p. 86). Bilingual pupils in language units tend to have more severe difficulties and progress slower than peers who speak one language (Crutchley *et al.*, 1997).

Teaching strategies for bilingual pupils with SEN may over-emphasise scripted direct teaching. This may lower the motivation of pupils and reduce their involvement because the teacher so predominantly initiates and controls language exchanges. The approach may also give insufficient attention to higher order conceptual skills (Cummins, 1984).

Cultural, ethnic and language differences form a context in which language difficulties can be understood and assessed (Martin, 2000). Approaches vary from teaching in English adapted to the pupils SEN to the interactive teaching of both the pupil's first language and English throughout the curriculum with adaptations according to the pupil's SEN (Cline, 1997).

Chapter 11

Assessment, recording and reporting

To meet the Professional Standards for Qualified Teacher Status, teachers must demonstrate that 'They make appropriate use of a range of monitoring and assessment strategies to evaluate pupils' progress towards planned learning objectives, and use this information to improve their own planning and teaching' (*QTS Standards*, TTA, 2002a, Chapter 3, section 2, sub-section 1).

'[T]rainees might use strategies such as observation, questioning, discussion and marking pupils' work in order to evaluate progress towards planned learning objectives' (*Handbook of Guidance on QTS Standards and ITT Requirements*, TTA, 2002b, Chapter 3, section 2, sub-section 1, evidence).

Teachers must demonstrate that 'They record pupils' progress and achievements systematically to provide evidence of the range of their work, progress and attainment over time. They use this to help pupils review their own progress and to inform planning' (*QTS Standards*, TTA, 2002a, Chapter 3, section 2, sub-section 6).

Trainees might demonstrate evidence of meeting QTS Standard 3.2.6 by 'making effective use of the school's existing record keeping systems' (Handbook of Guidance on QTS Standards and ITT Requirements, TTA, 2002b, Chapter 3, section 2, sub-section 6).

'They are able to use records as a basis for reporting on pupils' attainment and progress orally and in writing, concisely, informatively and accurately, for parents, carers, other professionals and pupils' (QTS Standards, TTA, 2002a, Chapter 3, section 2, sub-section 7).

'Trainees might also, with support, and if the opportunity arises, report orally to parents and carers on the progress of their children. Trainees will also need to show evidence that they are able to report on pupils' progress, should the need arise, to other professionals such as SEN Co-ordinators, educational psychologists and other colleagues when pupils change classes or transfer to a different school' (Handbook of Guidance on QTS Standards and ITT Requirements, TTA, 2002b, Chapter 3, section 2, sub-section 7, evidence).

This chapter considers ways of assessing, recording and reporting progress and attainment for pupils with SEN. The chapter begins by touching on some general points about assessment, recording and reporting that apply to all schools and all children. It then considers assessment and recording relating to the curriculum, the use of Performance Descriptors and the curriculum, and assessment and recording through teaching. It outlines a practical way of assessing and recording progress and achievement for pupils with SEN, taking account of other factors such as gender and ethnicity. Finally, the chapter considers the various people for whom assessment information is of interest (pupils, parents, and professionals) and how they might be involved.

Assessment, recording and reporting in general

It may be helpful to consider some general suggestions and observations about assessment, recording and reporting before concentrating on pupils with SEN:

> Assessment arrangements for national school tests and tasks and teacher assessment seem to be forever changing and becoming more complex and interdependent . . . The importance of the assessment of pupil attainment is unquestioned and its relationship with benchmarking and target setting and with value added measures can only increase its profile.
>
> (Farrell, 1999, p. 10)

> It is to be hoped that national tests and task procedures will be gradually stabilised and simplified. They may then form a secure and integral part of the school's battery of assessment information to be used to inform classroom organisation, teaching approaches and other aspects of teaching and learning. In this way their value will be enhanced and their important role in conveying to parents and others the overall standards of the school will be retained.
>
> (Ibid., p. 13)

> Gathering information should be as economical as possible both in terms of financial costs and time . . . Recording the information too should be as economical as ingenuity can make it.
>
> (Farrell, 2001a, p. 6)

The above observations happened to refer mainly to national test and tasks. In 1999 when the observation in the second of the above quotes was made, it seemed reasonable to hope that national tests and task procedures would be gradually stabilised and simplified for the majority of children. Recent developments such as the refinement and wider use of Performance Descriptors (Department for Education and Employment/QCA, 2001) make similar aspirations realistic for those children with SEN who may be achieving below level 1 of the National Curriculum, for example, at the end of Key Stage 2. Naturally the remit of assessment and of related recording and reporting extends much wider than national tests and it is to some of these other forms of assessment and recording that we now turn.

Assessment and recording relating to the curriculum

It is important that the curriculum-related assessment of pupils with SEN forms part of and emerges from the general assessments used in the whole school. This enables the attainment and progress of pupils with SEN to be seen in the context of that of other pupils and it also allows extra and more detailed assessments for pupils with SEN to be made as necessary. Accordingly, the broad achievements of pupils with SEN would as appropriate be known in terms of the following:

- the Foundation Stage Profile statutory assessment;
- National Curriculum levels in each subject;
- objectives in the National Numeracy and National Literacy Frameworks.

Assessments might also be carried out and recorded using tools sensitive to finer gradations of progress. These could include:

- Performance Descriptors relating to levels below National Curriculum level 1;
- standardised tests;
- video recordings of subtle interactions perhaps for pupils with severe communication difficulties;
- developmental checklists;
- the progress indicated by progressive targets on successive Individual Education Plans (particularly if these are related to the progress of a cohort of pupils with similar SEN working from a similar level of prior learning).

Also, for pupils with a statement of SEN, assessment and recording would be facilitated by the statement itself, and information from annual reviews as well as IEPs.

All such assessments may be related closely to the curriculum to help ensure that there are high educational aspirations for pupils with SEN.

Performance Descriptors and the curriculum

Performance Descriptors, as mentioned earlier, are one way of recognising progress and attainment. These are an aspect of an approach to planning, teaching and assessing pupils with SEN (Qualifications and Curriculum Authority, 2001a). Related guidelines include subject materials for the following:

• National Curriculum subjects;
• religious education;
• thinking skills and key skills;
• personal, social and health education and citizenship.

The approach includes a framework for recognising achievements below level 1 of the National Curriculum. The guidelines relate to all pupils aged 5 to 16 years with learning difficulties including pupils 'unlikely to achieve above level 2 at Key Stage 4' (pupils with severe learning difficulties or profound and multiple learning difficulties) and pupils 'who may be working at age related expectations in some subjects but are well below this in others' (pupils with moderate learning difficulties) (Ibid., p. 4).

The Performance Descriptors comprise eight steps (some of them sub-divided) in which steps one to three indicate general attainment and are common to all subjects. Performance Descriptor P1(i) for example is, 'Pupils encounter activities and experiences. They may be passive or resistant. They may show simple reflex responses, *for example startling at sudden noises or movements*. Any participation is fully prompted' (Qualifications and Curriculum Authority, 2001b, p. 29, italics in the original).

Performance Descriptors four to eight show subject-related attainment. For example, in the English subject guidelines Performance Descriptor P4 for 'reading' is 'Pupils listen and respond to familiar rhymes and stories. They show some understanding of how books work, *for example, turning pages and holding the book the right way up*' (Ibid., p. 31, italics in the original).

The Performance Descriptors may be employed in relation to assessment and recording. Teachers may use them to do the following:

• develop or support more focused day-to-day approaches to ongoing teacher assessment by using the descriptions to refine and develop long-, medium- and short-term planning;

- track linear progress towards subject-specific attainment at National Curriculum level 1;
- identify lateral progress by looking for related skills at similar levels across subjects;
- record pupils' overall development and achievement, for example, at the end of a year or a key stage;
- decide which description best fits a pupil's performance over a period of time and in different contexts, using their professional judgement.

(Qualifications and Curriculum Authority, 2001a, p. 28)

Assessment and recording through teaching

In teaching, the use of short-term plans (STP), that is, weekly plans and lesson plans, can be effectively linked to assessment. The STP indicates the learning outcomes for the whole class and for groups within it. Varied teaching approaches and other interventions address the learning outcomes. The extent to which these are achieved is recorded and feeds into the STP for the following week.

A learning outcome might be that a pupil or a small group of pupils demonstrate some understanding of the concept 'one' in number by giving an object from a group of identical objects when asked, 'Please give me one' (see Qualifications and Curriculum Authority, 2001c, Performance Indicator 5 in 'number', p. 23 for similar activities). A pupil might touch one object in response to the request but not despite prompts pick it up or hand it over.

A learning objective in subsequent STP might be to give the pupil a single item and request that he gives it to the teacher to allow teaching of 'picking up' and 'giving' which the child may not have understood or may have found difficult. This might later lead to the child being able to respond to the original task. This forms a cycle of learning outcome, pupil response, assessment, and subsequent modified learning outcome which informs both teaching and assessment.

Assessing and recording the progress of pupils with SEN taking account of other factors

Factors such as gender and ethnicity can inform the interpretation of data on the achievement and progress of pupils with SEN.

When assessing the attainment and progress of pupils with SEN, it is helpful to consider issues such as gender and ethnicity. As an example, consider the use of achievement data on reading assessed over a specified period of time. Each pupil with SEN will have a score indicating standards of reading and, if parallel tests are made over a certain time scale, this will also provide an indication of progress.

Next, one considers pupil factors that might have a bearing on standards and progress of pupils with SEN. These include gender, ethnicity, main learning difficulty, social background, and age.

In looking at standards and progress at the school level, if we take the example of gender, the data on reading standards would be set out so that the scores for boys and girls could be compared. The average rate of progress of boys and girls could also be scrutinised. Let us assume that in a particular school the figures for the current standards in reading indicate that boys score significantly lower than girls. The average progress over perhaps six months is then determined by deducting previous scores from current scores and separating the figures for boys and girls. This indicates that the average progress of boys is lower than that for girls.

One can then examine possible influential factors. Among these may be that the resources used in the school capture the interest of girls more than boys. The gender composition of staff (perhaps particularly influential staff or senior staff) may be predominantly female, so boys with SEN do not have many male role models in the school. Out-of-school or lunchtime clubs for reading may be attracting predominantly girls. There may be a tendency in the school for boys to regard reading as uninteresting or unappealing.

Once the school has examined the plausible reasons for the assessment data on reading, it can consider the possible provision to address the apparent discrepancies between boys and girls. The school could review the resources used, auditing those appealing to boys and establishing what materials boys would find more interesting than what is available. It could then plan the relocation of resources or the purchase or loan of other resources to rectify this. Long-term staffing policy could aim within the law on equal opportunities to recruit more male members of staff, particularly in senior positions.

In the shorter and medium term, the school could ensure that visiting staff or others such as artists or sculptors or storytellers include male role models. If parents who are helping at the school are mainly or exclusively mothers, the school could examine ways of attracting fathers. The reasons why out-of-school or lunchtime clubs for reading particularly attract girls could be examined and strategies developed to interest and retain the membership of boys too. The factors behind the tendency in the school for boys to regard reading as uninteresting or unappealing could be explored by discussing this with boys and seeking ways to engage their interest.

A similar approach may be taken with reference to ethnicity, main learning difficulty, the child's social background and age. It would be equally easy to use numeracy scores or the scores from tests and assessments of speaking and listening. Also, perhaps with advice from an educational psychologist, assessments of behaviour, emotional development and social skills could be used. Other assessments such as Performance Descriptors (Qualifications and Curriculum Authority, 2001a) could be utilised depending on the purpose of the data collection. This approach demonstrates the standards and progress of pupils with SEN. It also enables the school to consider sub-groups within the wider group of pupils with SEN to examine whether there are further factors inhibiting standards of achievement and progress (for a fuller account, see Farrell, 2001b).

Reporting

Given that assessment information has been systematically gathered over a period of time and routinely recorded, it can be reported to different, 'audiences'. Pupils are not really the audience for the recorded information for, where possible, they will have been participants in the assessment, recording and reporting process. For example, the point of an IEP would be explained to a pupil and the teacher would reach agreement about the targets and strategies to be used to engage the pupil's fullest understanding and participation. As the teacher records that progressive targets have been reached in successive IEPs, the pupil will be involved in the recording of the progress that is represented.

Reporting progress to parents is done in the context of parents being partners in the education of their child. Such reporting will draw on the same information as that with which the pupil has been involved. In speaking to parents and in writing letters and reports intended for them, the teacher will try to avoid jargon and will be careful to make clear the child's strengths as well as areas of weakness.

Regarding areas of weakness, the teacher should indicate the strategies that are being used or planned and what targets will be used to monitor progress. Reporting to parents, particularly face to face, provides the teacher with an opportunity to listen to the parents' perspective and any concerns they may have.

Reporting will also include recognition of progress that the child has made and reference to any targets that have already been reached. The overall picture should be accurate, honest, should balance strengths and weakness and should look to the future. Comments should be based on clear evidence.

Although it has been suggested that jargon is avoided when communicating with parents, when reporting to professionals, there is no reason why jargon cannot be minimised. From time to time, however, perhaps jargon and acronyms are inevitable as a sort of professional shorthand. The information provided by the teacher will sometimes be tailored to the particular professional concerned. For example, the teacher may be consulting the SENCO to decide whether a child might require School Action intervention. In this case the SENCO will require evidence of the teaching strategies that have been used. They will also need evidence (usually in terms of records of progress) that, although the teaching strategies were appropriate, progress has been insufficient.

Chapter 12

Partners and participants

To meet the Professional Standards for Qualified Teacher Status, teachers must demonstrate that 'They can communicate sensitively and effectively with parents and carers, recognising their roles in pupils' learning, and their rights, responsibilities and interests in this' (*QTS Standards*, TTA, 2002a, Chapter 1, section 4).

In relation to partnerships with other professionals, teachers must demonstrate that 'They understand the contribution that support staff and other professionals make to teaching and learning' (*QTS Standards*, TTA, 2002a, Chapter 1, section 6).

One aspect of Standard 1.6 is 'the trainee teacher's understanding of the distinct roles of other professionals including, for example, social workers, educational psychologists, education welfare officers, youth justice workers, school nurses or other health professionals' (*Handbook of Guidance on QTS Standards and ITT Requirements*, TTA, 2002b, Chapter 1, section 6).

Teachers must demonstrate that 'They understand their responsibilities under the SEN Code of Practice, and know how to seek advice from specialists on less common types of special educational needs' (*QTS Standards*, TTA, 2002a, Chapter 2, section 6).

QTS Standard 2.6, 'Trainees should know how to access the advice they need to support the learning needs of pupils with SEN and disabilities, and be aware of the sources of advice likely to be available to them outside the school – for example, via the internet, from the LEA SEN support services, special schools, health professionals and voluntary organisations. Trainees will not be expected to have the same level of expertise as experienced teachers of the SENCO, or to draw up an IEP independently' (*Handbook of Guidance on QTS Standards and ITT Requirements*, TTA, 2002b, Chapter 2, section 6, scope).

'They take part in, and contribute to, teaching teams as appropriate to the school. Where applicable, they plan for the deployment of additional adults who support pupils' learning' (*QTS Standards*, TTA, 2002a, Chapter 3, section 1, sub-section 4).

'They work collaboratively with specialist teachers and other colleagues and, with the help of an experienced teacher as appropriate, manage the work of teaching assistants or other adults to enhance pupils' learning' (*QTS Standards*, TTA, 2002a, Chapter 3, section 3, sub-section 13).

'Trainees will demonstrate in their planning and teaching, often in a variety of contexts, that they are able to manage the work of, for example, teaching assistants, parents, volunteers, and/or LSAs to enhance learning opportunities for pupils' (*Handbook of Guidance on QTS Standards and ITT Requirements*, TTA, 2002b, Chapter 3, section 3, sub-section 13, evidence).

To meet *Induction Standards* (i) NQTs should, by the end of their induction period, 'liaise effectively with parents and carers on pupils' progress and achievements'.

> To meet *Induction Standards* (m) NQTs should, 'as relevant to the post in which they are completing induction, effectively and appropriately deploy, liaise with and manage other adults who support pupils' learning in and outside the classroom' (*Induction Standards*, TTA, 2002c).

This chapter first considers the role of parents of pupils with SEN including being informed that their child has SEN, and their involvement in statutory assessment and annual reviews of statements of SEN. This draws on the role of parents as envisaged in the *Special Educational Needs Code of Practice* (Department for Education and Skills, 2001a) and in the *SEN Toolkit* (Department for Education and Skills, 2001b, 2001c). The chapter considers communications between the parent and teacher, mentions the Independent Panel for Special Educational Advice (IPSEA) as an example of an advocacy organisation and gives an example of a local parent partnership scheme.

It then examines the role of governors and of professionals involved in supporting pupils with SEN. The chapter discusses in particular the teaching assistant, the educational psychologist, the special needs officer, the advisor responsible for NQTs, the education welfare officer, the social worker and the speech and language therapist. Finally, the chapter looks at the most important participant in the child's education, the child himself.

Parents

Under the *Special Educational Needs Code of Practice* (Department for Education and Skills, 2001a), to fulfil their roles effectively, LEAs should monitor and review the role and quality of parent partnership services (Ibid., Chapter 1, section 15).

Parents should be supported to be able to and to be empowered to do the following:

- recognise and fulfil their responsibilities as parents and play an active and valued role in their child's education;
- have knowledge of their child's entitlement within the SEN framework;

- make their views known about how their child is educated;
- have access to information, advice and support during assessment and any related decision-making process about special educational provision.

(Ibid., Chapter 2, section 2)

Suggestions to make communications with parents effective include that professionals should 'acknowledge and draw on parental knowledge and expertise in relation to their child' and 'respect the differing needs parents themselves may have, such as a disability, or communication and linguistic barriers' (Ibid., Chapter 2, section 7).

The *Code* provides guidance relating to schools working in partnership with parents (Ibid., Chapter 2, sections 10–11), supporting parents during statutory assessment (Ibid., Chapter 2, section 12) and LEAs working in partnership with parents (Ibid., Chapter 2, sections 13–14). It recognises the contribution of the voluntary sector, advising that 'LEAs and schools should regularly involve the voluntary sector in consultations, training days and information exchanges' (Ibid., Chapter 2, section 15).

LEAs must make arrangements for parent partnership services, informing parents, schools, and others about the arrangements for the service and how they can gain access to it. LEAs must 'remind parents about the parent partnership service and the availability of disagreement resolution services at the time a proposed statement or amended notice is issued' (Ibid., Chapter 2, section 16).

Minimum standards are set out that LEAs and parent partnership services are expected to follow in delivering effective parent partnership services (Ibid., Chapter 2, sections 18 and 21). Minimum standards are similarly set out for an effective disagreement resolution service (Ibid., Chapter 2, section 25). A useful table, which readers may wish to consult, outlines the roles and responsibilities of LEAs, the voluntary sector, schools and parent partnership services (Ibid., p. 26).

In early education settings, it is recognised that a parent's perspective is particularly important when assessing the SEN of young children. LEAs should consider using leaflets or guidelines for parents that encourage their participation (Ibid., Chapter 4, section 40). In the primary phase (Ibid., Chapter 5, section 14) and in the secondary sector (Ibid., Chapter 6, section 13), 'Schools should also be open and responsive to expressions of concern by parents and take account of any information that parents provide about their child.'

Regarding the statutory assessment of SEN, the involvement of parents is important. Before deciding whether to make such an assessment requested by a school or other agency, the LEA has to follow certain procedures, such as writing to parents to give them notice that the LEA is considering whether to make a statutory assessment (Ibid., Chapter 7, section 16). If a parent requests a statutory assessment, the LEA has to comply unless they have made a statutory assessment within six months of the date of the request or unless they consider a statutory assessment unnecessary (having examined all the evidence provided to them) (Ibid., Chapter 7, section 21). For the purpose of making a statutory assessment, the LEA must seek written parental advice as well as educational, medical, psychological and social services advice (Ibid., Chapter 7, section 82).

If the LEA decide not to issue a statement but issue a 'note in lieu' of one, then the LEA must write to parents informing them and giving the reasons. They must tell parents of the right of appeal against the decision to the SEN and Disability Tribunal and other matters (Ibid., Chapter 8, section 15).

On receiving a proposed statement, parents have the right to express a preference for the maintained school their child should attend and to make representations to the LEA and hold meeting with LEA officers and others (Ibid., Chapter 8, section 57). The involvement of parents in the process of making a statement of SEN is set out in Chapter 8 of the *Code*.

Concerning the annual review of statements, the head teacher convening the meeting must invite the child's parents as well as a relevant teacher, a representative of the placing LEA, a person whom the LEA considers appropriate, and any other person the head teacher considers appropriate (Ibid., Chapter 9, section 16).

In short, the *Code* envisages an important role for the parents of children with SEN and this is underpinned at certain points by statutory requirements to ensure that parents are involved and properly informed.

The *SEN Toolkit* develops some of the issues in the *Code*, particularly the booklets section 2 (Department for Education and Skills, 2001b) and section 3 (Department for Education and Skills, 2001c).

Communicating with parents

In communicating with parents, the trainee and newly qualified teacher might keep in mind the important contribution that parents can make to the education of their child. Parents have knowledge and information about their child which may not be apparent in the school setting but which may have a bearing on the child's learning. They can make invaluable contributions by working closely with the school, working as one with the school and supporting homework. This does not imply of course that every parent wishes to work in partnership with the school or is able to.

When meeting parents, the teacher needs to prepare carefully, ensuring that he or she has evidence, such as the child's work, for any points that he or she wishes to raise. The meeting may include important elements such as: explaining the work that has already been done and the support that has been given, the positive things that the child has achieved, the causes of concern, and the provisional strategies that are being considered to address the SEN. The teacher will then want to listen to the views of the parents concerning the issues raised and anything else that they wish to contribute. The meeting may involve discussing learning targets that the child will work towards. The teachers will make a written note of the discussion. This may be followed up as necessary with a letter to parents confirming what has been said and what has been agreed.

Teachers in training and newly qualified teachers may find it particularly helpful to become familiar with some of the organisations that support parents of children with SEN. Time taken to familiarise oneself with the sorts of issues with which these organisations deal will help teachers to better understand the perspective of some parents.

One example is the Independent Panel for Special Educational Advice (IPSEA) which is a volunteer-based organisation offering help to parents of children with special needs who are having problems with their education. It offers free independent advice on LEAs' legal duties to assess and provide for children with SEN. IPSEA provides a source of long-term advice and advocacy. It offers, when necessary, advice on the statutory assessment and statement process, home visits, help at meetings, and advice and representation at SEN and disability tribunal appeals (see: http://www.ipsea.org.uk).

Local parent partnership services offer another useful perspective. For example, Tameside Parent Partnership Service aims to provide parents with a range of services enabling them to be better informed about SEN procedures and provision allowing parents to take a more active and informed role in their child's education. It offers independent advice, guidance and support to the parents of children with SEN (http://www.tameside.gov.uk/corpgen2/parentpart.htm).

The work of others involved in supporting pupils with SEN

Governors

The duties of governing bodies are summarised in the *Special Educational Needs Code of Practice* (Department for Education and Skills, 2001a, e.g. Chapter 1, sections 16–22). With the head teacher, governing bodies 'decide the school's general policy and approach to meeting pupils' special educational needs'. They should establish 'appropriate staffing and funding arrangements and oversee the school's work' (Ibid., Chapter 1, section 16).

Governors of community, voluntary and foundation schools and LEAs in relation to maintained nursery schools must 'do their best to ensure that the necessary provision is made for pupils with special educational needs' (Ibid., Chapter 1, section 17).

A particular governor may be given particular responsibility to oversee SEN and all governors, especially any such SEN governors, should make sure that they are 'up to date and knowledgeable about the school's SEN provision, including how funding, equipment and personnel are deployed' (Ibid., Chapter 1, section 22).

There are also useful general guides for governors (e.g. Gordon and Williams, 2002) that will help the teacher understand the governors' perspective and aid communication with them.

The range of professionals

Among other professionals working with pupils with SEN who are usually external to the school are the following:

- educational psychologist
- special needs officer
- support teacher
- social worker
- medical doctor
- nurse
- speech and language therapist
- occupational therapist
- child protection officer
- educational welfare officer
- SEN advisor or inspector
- peripatetic specialist SEN teacher
- Connexions personal adviser (in secondary sector).

This list is far from exhaustive and the roles of these professionals and others are described in other publications (e.g. Farrell, 2002). The new teacher is likely to come into contact with some other professionals when attending an annual review of a child's state- ment as the class teacher in primary school or sometimes (with the SEN Co-ordinator) as a subject teacher in secondary school. Often the educational psychologist and a special needs officer attend at least some of these meetings. New teachers will also meet other professionals at in-service training sessions organised by the LEA or others.

It is helpful to be clear about the roles of other colleagues and of what they can and cannot do so that one develops realistic but ambitious expectations of others. The SENCO is usually the person facilitating access to these staff for the new teacher. To illustrate the importance of understanding the roles of colleagues, Let us briefly look at the roles of the teaching assistant, the educa- tional psychologist and several other professionals.

The teaching assistant

In studying four schools (Clarke *et al.*, 1999), in-class support was found to be the most used way of encouraging inclusion. However, it was not possible to support every class that a pupil with SEN attended so the approach was not able to be compre- hensive. Also the relationships between teacher and teaching assis- tant were not uniformly productive. Teachers sometimes resented the 'intrusion' of a teaching assistant, roles were often unclear, and effective shared planning was rare.

Garner and Davies (2001) provide a useful summary of some of the main duties of the teaching assistant. The activities of the teaching assistant include the following:

- helping the teacher to plan children's work; to organise the classroom to enable differentiated work; to prepare curriculum materials; with particular pupil tasks with individual pupils; to keep children on task;
- making suggestions about curriculum content;
- working with individuals or groups of children;
- contributing to and supporting the child's IEP;
- providing additional explanations to children;
- supporting the teacher in general behaviour management;
- reviewing individual pupil progress in collaboration with the teacher;
- attending school briefings and professional development sessions;
- liaising with parents where appropriate.

Within the school, it is important that the teacher works closely with teaching assistants (sometimes called learning support assistants). While a teaching assistant may not work exclusively with pupils with SEN, he or she needs an understanding of children with SEN just as a teacher does. A teaching assistant working with pupils with SEN should liaise closely with the teacher. Joint planning is the ideal but, failing this, the teacher should convey to the teaching assistant the learning objectives of the lesson and the learning outcomes expected of the pupil(s) being supported as well as the teaching and support strategies to be used. Assessments of what the pupil has done should be recorded so as to inform subsequent teaching. The teacher should ensure that he or she does not lose the skill of working with pupils with SEN because their needs are met too readily by the involvement of a teaching assistant.

The educational psychologist

The aims of the educational psychologist and key principles, success factors and core functions were set out in *Educational*

Psychology Service (England): Current Role, Good Practice and Future Directions: Report of the Working Group (Department for Education and Employment, 2000a) and in a related research report (Department for Education and Employment, 2000b). The expectations of others were considered and how they relate to what educational psychologists (EPs) want. Ways in which the expectations of other people might be managed by particular educational psychology services were outlined.

The educational psychology team often represents a rich source of expertise and skill which the LEA may not always tap to its full potential. When EPs are restricted too much to preparing statutory assessments and statements, they often feel that this potential is wasted. While this is widely recognised, the implications are not always followed through. These are to review the process of making statements and to recognise the cost of statements and the bureaucracy supporting them and seek other ways to deliver support for SEN.

This is likely for some time to involve a system like statementing. However, the extent of the use of statements and finding the time for EPs to employ their skills in early intervention and other areas are challenging. Approaching this issue across the whole of the LEA is likely to lead to a more efficient deployment of resources for SEN and greater job satisfaction for EPs. This in turn is likely to lead to better recruitment and retention of EPs and better continuity of service to parents, children and schools.

For the newly qualified teacher, contact with the EP may arise through the EP offering advice on a pupil's learning and development, Individual Education Plans and learning targets; observing a pupil in lessons; and attendance at an annual review of a child's statement.

The special needs officer (SNO)

The role of SNOs includes that of case workers, named officers and statement writers and as representatives of the LEA at annual reviews of statements. The case worker role may include liaising with a multi-disciplinary panel who make decisions about statements of SEN and related issues. The named officer role particularly involves providing information for parents. The statement writing role may be fulfilled 'in house' by the SNOs or externally to the LEA by contracted statement writers. The LEA representative role at annual reviews may be shared with others such as educational psychologists.

The liaison work of SNOs is important to help ensure prompt response times from colleagues in the health services and social services when a statement of SEN is being collated. Organising expeditious translations of documents into languages other than English is sometimes necessary. The SNO makes use of information technology sytems to save time and to keep data retrieval manageable (Farrell, 2003).

The adviser responsible for newly qualified teachers

The general adviser for NQTs in a local education authority is responsible for the training of NQTs and induction tutors; for maintaining an overview of and supervising induction; and for monitoring a sample of NQTs to ensure that the induction standards are consistently applied. The adviser will determine with the headteacher whether or not the NQT has met the induction standards and will collaborate with LEA staff and professional organisations where there are difficulties between the NQT and the school or where the NQT is likely to fail induction.

The educational welfare officer (EWO)

The educational welfare officer, also known as the education social worker, is an LEA employee whose duties include ensuring that parents fulfil their child's right to education through attendance at school or through another appropriate means such as tuition at home. The EWO advises parents of their rights and liaises with other colleagues such as social workers, schools and educational psychologists. They deal with free school meals applications, license children for part-time employment, and work with excluded pupils. The EWO also offers advice and training to schools to develop an attendance policy and arranges alternative education for pupils not educated at school.

The social worker

The Children Act 1989 and the Education Act 1996 place duties on school, local education authorities, health services and the social services departments to help each other in taking action on behalf of children with SEN. Furthermore, the *Special Educational Needs Code of Practice* (Department for Education and Skills, 2001a) states that school-based stages of assessment will be effective where schools work closely with others, including social workers.

Within this framework, a social worker's role includes supporting people with disabilities and emotional, social and economic difficulties. Some social workers work particularly with children with SEN and their families.

The speech and language therapist

Among the health professionals with whom the new teacher may come into contact, when the pupils' SEN relates to communication difficuties, is the speech and language therapist (SALT). Speech and language therapy aims to enable those with speech and language and communication difficulties and related difficulties with eating and swallowing to communicate as well as possible and to achieve independence. The SALT works with children (and adults) assessing and treating communication difficulties through therapy and teaching. The SALT and the teacher need to liaise closely. SALTs may work as consultants to teachers and parents who participate in delivering the activities aimed at improving the child's communication. Should the National Health Service not provide speech and language therapy for a child whose statement specifies it as an educational provision, 'ultimate' responsibility for that provision rests with the LEA unless the child's parents have made other suitable arrangements (*Code*, Chapter 8, section 51).

The child as an educational participant

At the heart of the educational process is the child. The child with SEN (or any other child) is not seen as a partner in education in the same way as a parent and other professionals. But the involvement of the child and their contribution relating to their education are crucial. At the same time it is recognised that there is a balance to be struck. This is between, on the one hand, giving the child a voice and encouraging them to make informed decisions and, on the other, 'overburdening them with decision-making procedures where they have insufficient experience and knowledge to make appropriate judgements without additional support' (The Children Act 1999).

Among strategies aimed at enhancing the child's participation are being clear in communicating with the child the areas where there are learning difficulties, at the same time as showing what might be done to address them. Also, explaining any assessment used and why it is being used; drafting Individual Education Plans in co-operation with the child and explaining the strategies and the targets; explaining the aims of any intervention and explaining how it will be monitored to check if it is working. Where other professionals are involved such as a speech and language therapist or a physiotherapist, ensuring that the child understands their role. Child advocacy services may be used.

Appendix I

Useful addresses

ADD/ADHD Family Support
Group
1a High Street
Dilton Marsh
Westbury
Wilts BA13 4DL
Tel: 01373 826 045

Advisory Centre for Education
1b Aberdeen Studios
22 Highbury Grove
London N5 2DQ
Tel: 0207 354 8318

British Dyslexia Association
98 London Road
Reading
Berkshire RG1 5AU
Tel: 0118 966 8271

British Educational
Communications Technology
Agency (BECTA)
Milburn Hill Road
Science Park
Coventry
CV4 7JJ
Tel: 024 7641 6994

Centre for Studies in Inclusive
Education
1 Redland Close
Elm Lane
Redland
Bristol BS6 6UE
Tel: 0117 923 8450

Department for Education
and Skills Publications
Centre
PO Box 5050
Sherwood Park
Annesley
Nottingham NG15 0DJ
Tel: 0845 602 2260

Dyslexia Institute
133 Gresham Road
Staines
Middlesex TW18 6UE
Tel: 01784 463851

Dyspraxia Foundation
8 West Alley
Hitchin
Herts SG5 1EG
Tel: 01462 454986

Education Management
Information Exchange (EMIE)
National Foundation for
Educational Research
The Mere
Upton Park
Slough
Berkshire SL1 2DQ
Tel: 01753 574 123

National Association for
Special Educational Needs
NASEN House
4/5 Amber Business Village
Amber Close
Amington
Tamworth
Staffs B77 4RP
Tel: 01827 311500

National Autistic Society
393 City Road
London EC1V 1NG
Tel: 0207 833 2299

OFSTED Publication Centre
PO Box 6927
London E3 3NZ
Tel: 0207 510 0180

QCA Publications
PO Box 99
Sudbury
Suffolk CO10 2SN
Tel: 01787 884444

Special Educational Needs
Joint Initiative for Training
Institute of Education
University of London
20 Bedford Way
London WC1H 0AL
Tel: 0207 612 6305

Special Educational Needs
Tribunal
7th Floor
Windsor House
50 Victoria Street
London SW1H 0NW
Tel: 0207 925 6925

Teacher Training Agency
Publications Unit
Freepost ANG2037
Chelmsford
Essex CM1 1ZY
Tel: 0845 606 0323

Appendix 2

Internet addresses

The Internet addresses below will introduce you to some of the thousands of sites available relating to SEN. Where it is not self-evident what the organisation offers, a brief annotation is given.

For any Internet site, where a physical address is not given and where information is not credited to a particular known organisation or person, the information should not be taken at face value.

Advisory Centre for Education
Independent advice for parents.
www.ace-ed.org.uk

British Educational Communications Technology Agency (BECTA)
Develops and promotes the use of information and communications technology in education and training.
www.becta.org.uk

Contact-a-family
Provides advice and support to parents whatever the medical condition of their child. Directory of rare and specific disorders.
www.cafamily.org.uk

Education Quest
Analyses news on education in Britain and abroad. For schools, colleges, universities, teachers, parents and pupils. The section 'special education' lists other sites.
www.education-quest.com

Inclusive Technology Ltd.
Special needs articles and information.
www.inclusive-technology.com/infosite/snhome.sntml

Independent Panel for Special Educational Advice
Help for parents of children with special needs
www.ipsea.org.uk

National Association for Special Educational Needs (NASEN)
www.nasen.org.uk

National Foundation for Educational Research
www.nfer.ac.uk

National Grid for Learning
Various SEN sites under 'search' SEN.
www.ngfl.gov.uk/ngfl/index.html

Office for Standards in Education
www.ofsted.gov.uk

Qualifications and Curriculum Authority
www.qca.org.uk

Teacher Training Agency
www.teach-tta.gov.uk/index.htm

Glossary

Advocacy Usually involves a nominated person speaking and acting on behalf of a person with SEN to try to secure rights or facilities.

Annual review A review of a statement of SEN.

Behaviour support plan An LEA plan setting out arrangements concerning the education of children with behaviour difficulties.

Connexions Service A service working with children aged 13–19 to help them optimise educational/vocational choices and prepare for the successful transition to work and adulthood.

Individual Education Plan A working document concerning planning, teaching and monitoring progress. It is used at Early Year/School Action, Early Years Plus/School Action Plus, and for pupils with statements.

Performance Descriptors Set out assessment criteria for attainment leading to level 1 of the National Curriculum.

Pupil Referral Unit An establishment intended to provide short-term support for pupils before their expected reintegration into mainstream schools.

Special Educational Needs Disability Tribunal A body hearing appeals against a decision made by an LEA regarding statutory assessments or statements of SEN.

Statement of SEN A document prepared by an LEA made when the LEA decides that the provision necessary to meet a child's SEN cannot reasonably be provided within the resources that are normally available to ordinary schools in its area.

Statutory assessment An assessment of a child's SEN by an LEA that may result in a statement of SEN being issued.

Bibliography

Ainscow, M. (1999) *Understanding the Development of Inclusive Schools*, London: Falmer Press.

Bailey, J. (1998) 'Australia; inclusion through categorisation', in T. Booth and M. Ainscow (eds) *From Them to Us: An International Study of Inclusion in Education*, London: Routledge.

Ballard, K. (1995) 'Inclusion, paradigms, power and participation', in C. Clarke, A. Dyson and A. Millward (eds) *Towards Inclusive Schools?*, London: David Fulton Publishers.

Barton, L. (1995) 'The politics of education for all', *Support for Learning*, 10, 4, 156–160.

Berger, A., Henderson, J. and Morris, D. (1999) *Implementing the Literacy Hour for Pupils with Learning Difficulties*, London: David Fulton.

Booth, T. and Ainscow, M. (1998) *From Them to Us: An International Study of Inclusion in Education*, London: Routledge.

Booth, T., Ainscow, M., Black-Hawkins, K., Vaughn, M. and Shaw, L. (2000) *Index for Inclusion: Developing Learning and Participation in Schools*, Bristol: Centre for Studies in Inclusive Education.

British Psychological Society (1999) *Dyslexia, Literacy and Psychological Assessment*, Leicester: BPS.

Brooks, G. (2002) *What Works for Children with Learning Difficulties? The Effectiveness of Intervention Schemes*, London: Department for Education and Skills.

Centre for Studies on Inclusive Education (undated) brochure *Inclusive Education: The Right to Belong to the Mainstream*, Bristol: CSIE.

Centre for Studies on Inclusive Education (1999) *The Inclusion Charter: Ending Segregation in Education for All Children and Young People with Disabilities and Learning Difficulties*, Bristol: CSIE.

Clarke, C., Dyson, A. Millward, A. and Robson, S. (1999) 'Theories of inclusion, theories of schools: deconstructing and reconstructing the inclusive school', *British Educational Research Journal*, 25(2), 157–177.

Cline, T. (1997) 'Special educational needs and language proficiency', in C. Leung and C. Cable (eds) *English as an Additional Language: Changing Perspectives*, Watford: National Association for Language Development in the Curriculum.

Croll, P. and Moses, D. (1985) *One in Five: The Assessment and Incidence of Special Educational Needs*, London: Routledge and Kegan Paul.

Croll, P. and Moses, D. (2000) 'Discussants' papers – Paper 3: Resources, policies and educational practice', in B. Norwich (ed.) *Policy Options Steering Group: Policy Option Paper 2* (3rd Series), Tamworth: National Association for Special Educational Needs.

Crutchley, A., Botting, N. and Conti-Ramsden, G. (1997a) 'Bilingualism and specific language impairment in children attending language units', *European Journal of Disorders of Communication*, 32, 267–276.

Crutchley, A., Conti-Ramsden, G. and Botting, N. (1997b) 'Bilingual children with specific language impairment and standardised assessment: preliminary findings from a study of children in language units', *International Journal of Bilingualism*, 1(2), 117–134.

Cummins, J. (1984) *Bilingualism and Special Education: Issues in Assessment and Pedagogy*, Clevedon: Multilingual Matters.

Daniels, H., Hey, V., Leonard, D. and Smith, M. (1999) 'Issues of equity in special needs education from a gender perspective', *British Journal of Special Education*, 26(4), 189–195.

Daniels, A. and Williams, H. (2000) 'Reducing the need for exclusions and statements for behaviour: The framework for intervention (Part 1)', *Educational Psychology in Practice*, 15(4), 220–227.

Department for Education and Employment (1997) *Excellence for All Children: Meeting Special Educational Needs*, London: DfEE.

Department for Education and Employment (1998a) *Meeting Special Educational Needs: A Programme of Action*, London: DfEE.

Department for Education and Employment (1998b) *The National Literacy Strategy: Framework for Teaching*, London: DfEE.

Department for Education and Employment (1999a) *Circular 10/99 Social Inclusion: Pupil Support*, London: DfEE.

Department for Education and Employment (1999b) *Circular 11/99 Social Inclusion: The LEA Role in Pupil Support*, London: DfEE.

Department for Education and Employment (1999c) *The National Numeracy Strategy: Framework for Teaching Mathematics from Reception to Year 6*, London: DfEE.

Department for Education and Employment (2000a) *Educational Psychology Service (England): Current Role, Good Practice and Future Directions – Report of the Working Group*, London: DfEE.

Department for Education and Employment (2000b) *Educational Psychology Service (England): Current Role, Good Practice and Future Directions – The Research Report*, London: DfEE.

Department for Education and Employment (2000c) *The Role of the Local Education Authority in School Education*, London: DfEE.

Department for Education and Employment (2000d) *SEN Code of Practice on the Identification and Assessment of Pupils with Special Educational Needs and SEN Thresholds: Good Practice Guidelines on Identification and Provision for Pupils with Special Educational Needs*, London: DfEE.

Department for Education and Employment (2001a) *Supporting the Target Setting Process (Revised March 2001): Guidance for Effective Target Setting for Pupils with Special Educational Needs*, London: DfEE.

Department for Education and Employment (2001b) *The Key Stage 3 National Strategy: Literacy Across the Curriculum*, London: DfEE.

Department for Education and Employment (2001c) *The Key Stage 3 National Strategy: Numeracy Teaching Units for Summer Schools*, London: DfEE.

Department for Education and Employment (2001d) *The Key Stage 3 National Strategy: Numeracy Across the Curriculum Notes for School Based Training* London: DfEE.

Department for Education and Employment/Department of Health (2000) *Guidance on the Education of Children and Young People in Public Care*, London: DfEE/DoH.

Department for Education and Employment/Qualifications and Curriculum Authority (1999a) *The National Curriculum: Handbook for Primary Teachers in England Key Stages 1 and 2*, London: DfEE/QCA.

Department for Education and Employment/Qualifications and Curriculum Authority (1999b) *The National Curriculum: Handbook for Secondary Teachers in England Key Stages 3 and 4*, London: DfEE/QCA.

Department for Education and Skills (2000) *Special Educational Needs Code of Practice* London: DFES

Department for Education and Skills (2000a) *Governors' Annual Reports and School Prospectuses in Primary Schools*, London: DfES.

Department for Education and Skills (2000b) *Governors' Annual Reports and School Prospectuses in Secondary Schools*, London: DfES.

Department for Education and Skills (2001a) *Special Educational Needs Code of Practice*, London: DfES.

Department for Education and Skills (2001b) *SEN Toolkit Section 2: Parent Partnership Services*, London: DfEE.

Department for Education and Skills (2001c) *SEN Toolkit Section 3: Resolution of Disagreements*, London: DfEE.

Department for Education and Skills (2001d) *SEN Toolkit-Section 5: Managing Individual Education Plans*, London: DfEE.

Department for Education and Skills (2001e) *The National Numeracy Strategy; Towards the National Curriculum for Mathematics: Examples of What Pupils with Special Educational Needs Should Be Able to Do at Each P Level*, London: DfES.

Department for Education and Skills (2002) *The Induction Period for Newly Qualified Teachers*, London: DfES.

Department of Health/Department of Education and Employment/Home Office (2000) *Framework for the Assessment of Children in Need and their Families*, London: The Stationery Office.

Deponio, P., Landon, J., Mullin, K. and Reid, G. (1999) 'An audit of the processes involved in identifying and assessing bilingual learners suspected of being dyslexic: a Scottish study', paper presented at the Multilingualism and Dyslexia: British Dyslexia Association International Conference, Manchester, 17–19 June.

Disability Rights Commission (2001a) *Draft Code of Practice (Schools) DRC: Special Educational Needs and Disability Act 2001*, London: The Stationery Office.

Disability Rights Commission (2001b) *Code of Practice (Post 16): New Duties from 2002 in the Provision of Post 16 Education and Related Services for Disabled People and Students*, London: The Stationery Office.

Dowling, E. and Osborne, E. (1994) *The Family and the School: A Joint Systems Approach to Problems with Children*, London: Routledge.

Farrell, M. (1999) *Key Issues for Primary Schools*, London: Routledge.

Farrell, M. (2001a) *Key Issues for Secondary Schools*, London: Routledge.

Farrell, M. (2001b) *Standards and Special Educational Needs*, London: Continuum.

Farrell, M. (2002) *Special Education Handbook*, 3rd edn, London: David Fulton Publishers.

Farrell, M. (2003) 'The role of the special needs officer', *Special Educational Needs Briefing*, Kingston upon Thames: Croner.

Farrell, M., Kerry, T. and Kerry, C. (1995) *The Blackwell Handbook of Education*, Oxford: Blackwell.

Frederickson, N., Frith, U. and Reason, R. (1997) *Phonological Assessment Battery*, Windsor: NFER-Nelson.

Frederickson, N. and Cline, T. (2002) *Special Educational Needs, Inclusion and Diversity: A Textbook*, Buckingham: Open University Press.

Garner, P. (2000) 'Pretzel only policy? Inclusion and the real world of teacher education', *British Journal of Special Education*, 27(3), 111–116.

Garner, P. (2001) 'Goodbye Mr Chips: special needs, inclusive education and the deceit of initial teacher training', in T. O'Brien (ed.) *Enabling Inclusion: Blue Skies . . . Dark Clouds*, London: The Stationery Office.

Garner, P. and Davies, J. D. (2001) *Introducing Special Educational Needs: A Companion Guide for Student Teachers*, London: David Fulton Publishers.

Gordon, M. and Williams, A. (2002) *Special Educational Needs and Disability in Mainstream School: A Governors' Guide*, Stafford: National Association of Special Educational Needs.

Gross, J., Berger, A. and Garnett, J. (1999) 'Special needs and the literacy hour: Some general principles', in A. Berger and J. Gross (eds) *Teaching the Literacy Hour in an Inclusive Classroom*, London: David Fulton Publishers.

Hall, D. (1995) *Assessing the Needs of Bilingual Pupils: Living in Two Languages*, London: David Fulton Publishers.

Harter, S. (1985) *Manual for the Self-Perception Profile for Children*, Denver, CO: University of Denver.

Kelly, B. (1999) 'Circle time: a systems approach to emotional and behavioural difficulties', *Educational Psychology in Practice*, 15(1), 40–44.

Keogh, B. K., Gallimore, R. and Weisner, T. (1997) 'A sociocultural perspective on learning and learning disabilities', *Learning Disabilities Research and Practice*, 12(2), 107–113.

Lingard, T. (2001) 'Does the Code of Practice help secondary SENCOs to improve learning?', *British Journal of Special Education*, 28(4), December.

Martin, D. (2000) 'Communication difficulties in a multicultural context', in J. Law, S. Parkinson, R. Tamhne (eds) *Communication Difficulties in Childhood: A Practical Guide*, Abingdon: Radcliffe Medical Press.

Mittler, P. (2000) *Working Towards Inclusion: Social Contexts*, London: David Fulton Publishers.

Moore, J. (2000) 'Developments in additional resources allocation to promote greater inclusion (SEN)', in B. Norwich (ed.) *Policy Options Steering Group: Policy Option Paper 2* (3rd Series), Tamworth: National Association for Special Educational Needs.

Mortimore, P., Sammons, P. and Echob, R. (1988) *School Matters: The Junior Years*, Salisbury: Open Books.

Mutter, V., Hulme, C. and Snowling, M. (1997) *Phonological Abilities Test*, London: The Psychological Corporation.

Norwich, B. (2000) 'Inclusion in education: from concepts, values and critique to practice', in H. Daniels (ed.) *Special Education Re-formed: Beyond Rhetoric?*, London: Falmer Press.

Office for Standards in Education (1999a) *Inspection of Newham Local Education Authority January 1999*, London: OfSTED.

Office for Standards in Education (1999b) *Special Education 1994–1998: A Review of Special Schools, Secure Units and Pupil Referral Units in England*, London: The Stationery Office.

Office for Standards in Education (1999c) *Handbook for Inspecting Primary and Nursery Schools with Guidance on Self-Evaluation*, London: OfSTED.

Office for Standards in Education (1999d) *Handbook for Inspecting Secondary Schools with Guidance on Self-Evaluation*, London: OfSTED.

Office for Standards in Education (2000) *Evaluating Educational Inclusion: Guidance for Inspectors and Schools*, London: OfSTED.

Office for Standards in Education (2002) *Information and Communications Technology: Effect of Government Initiatives: Pupils' Achievement*, London: OfSTED.

Ostad, S. A. (1997) 'Developmental differences in addition strategies: a comparison of mathematically disabled and mathematically normal children', *British Journal of Educational Psychology*, 67, 345–357.

Qualifications and Curriculum Authority (2001a) *Planning, Teaching and Assessing the Curriculum for Pupils with Learning Difficulties: General Guidelines*, London: QCA.

Qualifications and Curriculum Authority (2001b) *Planning, Teaching and Assessing the Curriculum for Pupils with Learning Difficulties: English*, London: QCA.

Qualifications and Curriculum Authority (2001c) *Planning, Teaching and Assessing the Curriculum for Pupils with Learning Difficulties: Mathematics*, London: QCA.

Qualifications and Curriculum Authority/Department for Education and Employment (2001) *Supporting the Target Setting Process: Guidance for Effective Target Setting for Pupils with Special Educational Needs*, London: QCA/DfEE.

Reid, M. K. and Borkowski, J. G. (1987) 'Causal attributions of hyperactive children: implications for teaching strategies and self-control', *Journal of Educational Psychology*, 79, 296–307.

Riddell, S. (1996) 'Gender and special educational needs', in G. Lloyd (ed.) *Knitting Progress Unsatisfactory: Gender and Special Issues in Education*, Edinburgh: Moray House Publications.

Riddell, S., Brown, S. and Duffield, J. (1994) 'Parental power and special educational needs: the case of specific learning difficulties', *British Educational Research Journal*, 20(3), 327–345.

Robertson, C. (1999) 'Initial teacher education and inclusive schooling', *Support for Learning*, 14(4), 169–173.

Rose, R. (2002) 'Primary school teacher perceptions of the conditions required to include pupils with special educational needs', *Educational Review*, 53(2), 147–155.

Schön, D. A. (1987) *Educating the Reflective Practitioner*, San Francisco: Jossey-Bass.

Slee, R. (1996) 'Disability, class and poverty: school structures and policing identities', in C. Christensen and F. Rizvi (eds) *Disability and the Dilemmas of Education and Justice*, Buckingham: Open University Press.

Snowling, M. (1998) 'Dyslexia as a phonological deficit: evidence and implications', *Child Psychology and Psychiatry Review*, 3(1), 4–11.

Solity, J. (1996) 'Discrepancy definitions of dyslexia: an assessment through teaching approach', *Educational Psychology in Practice*, 12(3), 141–151.

Stanovich, K. E. and Stanovich, P. J. (1997) 'Further thought on aptitude/ achievement discrepancy', *Educational Psychology in Practice*, 13(1), 3–8.

Teacher Training Agency (1998) *The National Standards for Special Educational Needs Co-ordinators*, London: TTA.

Teacher Training Agency (2002a) *Qualifying to Teach: Professional Standards for Qualified Teacher Status and Requirements for Initial Teacher Training*, London: TTA.

Teacher Training Agency (2002b) *Induction Standards (Draft Proposals for September 2002)*, London: TTA.

Teacher Training Agency (2002c) *Handbook of Guidance on QTS Standards and ITT Requirements*, London: TTA.

United Nations Educational, Scientific and Cultural Organisation (1994) *World Conference on Special Needs Education: Access and Quality*, Paris: UNESCO.

Wade, J. (1999) 'Including all learners: QCA's approach', *British Journal of Special Education*, 26(2), 80–82.

Winter, K. (1999) 'Speech and language therapy provision for bilingual children: aspects of the current service', *International Journal of Language and Communication Disorders*, 34(1), 85–98.

Author index

Ainscow, M. 26

Bailey, J. 27
Ballard, K. 27
Barton, L. 27
Berger, A. 69
Brooks G. 70
British Psychological Society 75–6

Centre for Studies on Inclusive
    Education 27
Clarke, C. 137
Cline, T. 118
Croll, P. 26, 117
Crutchley, A. 120
Cummins, J. 120

Daniels, H. 105
Department for Education and Skills
    (or past equivalent) 5, 11, 13, 22,
    26–9, 32, 37, 50, 54, 56, 59–61, 68,
    70–1, 74, 80, 82, 85, 90–1, 96, 100,
    106, 118, 132, 134, 136, 139, 141
Department of Health 21
Deponio, P. 120
Disability Rights Commission 18
Dowling, E. 105

Farrell, M. 22, 33, 48–9, 90, 96, 102,
    112, 123, 137, 140
Frederickson, N. 68, 72, 75–6, 105, 120

Garner, P. 138
Gross, J. 70

Harter, S. 103

Kelly, B. 105
Keogh, B. K. 117

Lingard, T. 61

Martin, D. 120
Mittler, P. 26
Moore, J. 26
Mortimer, P. 117
Mutter, V. 76

Norwich, B. 34

Office for Standards in Education 31,
    35, 62, 80, 94, 115
Ostad, S. A. 72

Qualifications and Curriculum
    Authority 125–6, 128

Reid, M. K. 104
Riddell, S. 116

Scoh, D. A. 112
Slee, R. 27
Snowling, M. 75
Solity, J. 76
Stanovich, K. E. 75

Teacher Training Agency 1–5, 8–9, 65,
    116

United Nations Educational, Scientific
    and Cultural Organisation 26

Wade, J. 28

Subject index

able pupils (very able pupils) 23
adapted keyboards 84
admission arrangements 19, 56
adviser for NQTs, 140
advocacy 142
annual report 56
assessment (specialist) 42
Assessment, recording and reporting:
  general, 123–4; and curriculum
  124; through teaching 126; and
  pupil progress 126–8; attainment
  34
autistic spectrum disorder 15

barriers to learning 30, 33–4, 44
behaviour 53, 60, 101–103
blind (see visual impairment)
Braille 87, 90

child: as educational participant 141–2;
  child care plan (CCP) 22
Circular 10/99 29
Circular 11/99 29
Class management 8
Code of Practice (SEN): general 13–17,
  37–46; and information and
  communications technology 82–83;
  and emotional and behavioural
  difficulties 106–8
cognition 15–16, 86
cognitive perspective of emotional,
  behavioural and social difficulties
  103–4
communication and interaction 14–15,
  85

deaf (see hearing impairment)
disability 12–13
discrimination 49
dyslexia 15, 75

early intervention 46
early years 39
early years action 38–9, 42
early years action plus 38–9, 42
Education Act (1996) 11
Educational Psychologist 138–9
Educational Welfare Service/Officer 140
emotional, social and behavioural
  difficulties 16, 64, 72, 86,
  100–108, 116
English as an additional language
  22–23, 118–120
Evaluating one's teaching 114
equal opportunity 47–50
ethnicity 117–8
Excellence for All Children (see Green
  Paper 1997)
Exclusion 20–1, 29
Expectations 59–60

Fair Funding 51
Foundation Stage 39

Gender 116–7
governors/governing body 54–6, 136
graduated response 91–2
'Green Paper' on SEN (1997) 27–8, 31

Health Service 137, 141
Hearing impairment 13, 16–17, 71

inclusion: definitions of 27–29; in
    mainstream 30–31; principles for
    32–4; and pupil attainment 34–5;
    social 29–30; and special schools
    31–32
Independent Panel for Special
    Educational Advice (IPSEA) 132,
    135–6
Index for Inclusion 30–31
Individual Educational Plan 42, 44,
    60–65, 71, 124, 128, 138, 142
Induction Standards 6–8
information and communications
    technology 80–86, 95

Key stage 3 strategy 73–4

learning difficulties/needs 12
Learning Support Assistant (see
    teaching assistant)
Lesson plans 115
literacy 68–71: and information and
    communications technology 84
literacy hour 70
Local Education Authority: general 39,
    91–4, 108, 133–6, 139; policy on SEN
    50–53
looked-after children 21–22

multi-sensory difficulties 16–17

National Curriculum: general 59, 72,
    113, 124–5; and inclusion 32–4; tests
    62
National Grid for learning 83
numeracy 71–72: and information and
    communications technology 85

observation: of other teachers 115–6
Office for Standards in Education
    (OfSTED): general 28, 62, 81–82;
    expectations regarding information
    and communications technology
    94–6
Out of school learning 65–66

parents/carers: general 41, 55, 72, 129,
    132–4; communicating with 135–6
partial hearing (see hearing impairment)
partial sight (see visual impairment)
partnership: with parents 132–6

performance descriptors: general 63,
    122–4, 128; -and curriculum 125–6
physical impairment/needs 16–17
profound and multiple learning
    difficulties 74
Programme of Action 28
progress of pupils 42–44, 126–8
psychodynamic perspectives of
    emotional, behavioural and social
    difficulties 74
pupil differences 116
pupil views 77

Qualified Teacher Status (QTS):
    professional standards for 3–5

reading 69–70
records/record keeping (see assessment,
    recording and reporting)
resources: range of 90–91; and
    graduated response 91–2; and
    statements of SEN 92–4; and Office
    for Standards in Education 94–6;
    and the classroom 96–7

School Action 43, 71, 106–108
School Action Plus 42–4, 71, 82, 93,
    106–108
Short term plans 126
sensory and physical needs 16–17, 86–7,
    96
social worker 140–141
speech and language therapist 88, 141
special educational needs: legal
    definition of 11–12
severe learning difficulties 74
special educational needs
    co-ordinator: consulting the 129;
    national standards for 45; role of 41,
    43, 45–6, 64, 91–2, 129, 137; and
    information and communications
    technology 82, 88
Special Educational Needs and
    Disability Act (2001) 18–21, 49
Special Educational Needs and
    Disability Tribunal (SENDIST) 18
special educational needs policy
SEN Toolkit 60–1, 132, 134: of LEA
    50–53; of school 54–5
special needs officer (SNO) 139–140
special schools 19, 31, 39

stereotyped views 49–50
specialist equipment 85–7
specific learning difficulties: in literacy
    75–7
standards of pupil achievement 59, 63
statement of SEN 33, 40, 92–4
statutory assessment 40, 82, 92–4
support services 136–141
switch control 84
systems perspective of emotional,
    behavioural and social difficulties
    104–5

target setting 62–3, 65
teacher: as practitioner researcher 112;
    responsibilities of 41–5

teaching: approaches 113–4; evaluating
    one's own 114–5; and effective
    practice 115–6
teaching assistants 70, 137–8
thresholds 68–9
triggers for intervention 42, 106–7

United Nations Educational, Scientific
    and Cultural Organisation
    (UNESCO) 26

Very able pupils 23
visual impairment 13, 17
voice recognition technology 83–4

word processor 84